The
Year
of the
Poet VI

August 2019

The Poetry Posse

inner child press, ltd.

The Poetry Posse 2019

Gail Weston Shazor

Shareef Abdur Rasheed

Teresa E. Gallion

hülya n. yılmaz

Kimberly Burnham

Tzemin Ition Tsai

Elizabeth Esguerra Castillo

Jackie Davis Allen

Joe Paire

Caroline 'Ceri' Nazareno

Ashok K. Bhargava

Alicja Maria Kuberska

Swapna Behera

Albert 'Infinite' Carrasco

Eliza Segiet

William S. Peters, Sr.

General Information

The Year of the Poet VI
August 2019 Edition

The Poetry Posse

1st Edition : 2019

Publisher Information
1st Edition : Inner Child Press
intouch@innerchildpress.com
www.innerchildpress.com

WHAT WOULD LIFE BE WITHOUT A LITTLE POETRY?

$\mathcal{D}$edication

This Book is dedicated to

Poetry . . .

The Poetry Posse

past, present & future

our Patrons and Readers

the Spirit of our Everlasting Muse

&

the Power of the Pen

to effectuate change!

In the darkness of my life
I heard the music
I danced . . .
and the Light appeared
and I dance

Janet P. Caldwell

Table of Contents

The Poetry Posse

Table of Contents . . . *continued*

August Featured Poets   111

Inner Child News   141

Other Anthological Works   163

Foreword

Southwest Asia, the westernmost region of Asia possesses a "crossroad of different cultures." The culture of Southwest Asia are most generally known as the cultures of the Middle East. The Arab World and Islamic World are the realm's two biggest cultural links.

Endowed with a rich history, several of the civilizations described by Arnold Toynbee in his survey of world history had their cradle in this exotic region. Many of the recorded events took place in towns like Jericho going back to 6800 B. C.

The great empires, Babylonian and the Assyrians, Persian Empires, and Arab Empire centered in Baghdad and Damascus, as well as that of the Turkish Ottomans.

The region consists of five largest ethnic groups: Arabs, Azebaijans, Kurds, Persians, and the Turks.

Many poems have been written as odes to the epic history enveloping the exotic region. The deserts alone make wonderful subjects depicting the desert nomads and their elusive, wandering way of life. Beautiful verses from the heart can be created after one discovers the melodramatic stories hidden in each place as accounts of time long gone resurface.

The Poetry Posse Family will take you to a beautiful cascade of memories and rhythmic compositions as we bring you with us to a delightful and enriching journey of the Arab World.

I hope you enjoy our diverse poetry offerings for this month of August.

Elizabeth Esguerra Castillo
International Author and Poet
Philippines

World Healing, World Peace 2020
International Poetry Symposium

Dear Friends & Family . . . Poets, Poetry Lovers & Humanitarians

We are so excited at ICPI, Inner Child Press International, as we have begun to mobilize for the upcoming epic event of the 'World Healing, World Peace 2020 Poetry Symposium'. Our plans are set for April of 2020. This event will be held in Atlantic City, New Jersey.

We are now collecting names, emails and telephone numbers for all potential resources that can make this event a highly successful, and one of significance that will have a resounding effect on our world and humanity at large. We are also looking for volunteers who can assist us in many areas of facilitation in the planning, staging and execution phases. Going forward, we will be speaking with the business, government, foundation and the private sectors for funding, sponsorship and suitable venues. So, if you know anything, or know someone, we welcome your input and insights.

We will begin shortly to put together our international guest list.

Communicate with us via our email at :

worldhealingworldpeace@gmail.com

or

intouch@innerchildpress.com

Visit our Web Site :

www.worldhealingworldpeacepoetry.com

Stay Tuned for the opening for submissions of World Healing World Peace 2020 Anthology. Opening for submissions September 1st 2019. All global citizens are welcome to submit. This anthology will be published and distributed April 2020.

Please share this information

Thank You

Inner Child Press International
'building bridges of cultural understanding'

www.innerchildpress.com

Preface

Dear Family and Friends,

Yes I am excited? This year we have aligned our vision with that of UNESCO as it honors and acknowledges a variety of Global Indigenous cultures. We are now in our sixth year of publication. As are on our way to hitting another milestone. Needless to say, I am elated. Our initial vision was to just perform at this level for the year of 2014. Since that time we have had the blessed opportunity to include many other wonderful word artists and storytellers in the Poetry Posse from lands, cultures and persuasions all over the world. We have featured hundreds of additional poets, thereby introducing their poetic offerings to our vast global readership.

In keeping with our effort and vision to expand the awareness of poets from all walks by making this offerings accessible, we at Inner Child Press International will continue to make every volume a FREE Download. The books are also available for purchase at the affordable cost of $7.00 per volume.

In the previous years, our monthly themes were Flowers, Birds, Gemstones, Trees and Past Cultures. This year we have elected to continue the

Cultural theme. In each month's volume you will have the opportunity to not only read at least one poem themed by our Poetry Posse members about such culture, but we have included a few words about the culture in our prologue. The reasoning behind this is that now our poetry has the opportunity to be educational for not only the reader, but we poets as well. We hope you find the poetic offerings insightful as we use our poetic form to relay to you what we too have learned through our research in making our offering available to you, our readership.

In closing, we would like to thank you for being an integral part of our amazing journey.

Enjoy our amazing featured poets . . . they are amazing!

Building Cultural Bridges of Understanding . . .

Bless Up . . . From the home in our hearts to yours

Bill

The Poetry Posse
Inner Child Press Ineternational

PS

Do Not forget about the World Healing, World Peace Poetry effort.

Available here

www.worldhealingworldpeacepoetry.com

For Free Downloads of Previous Issues of The Year of the Poet

www.innerchildpress.com/the-year-of-the-poet

poetry is . . . .

Southwest Asia

Southwest Asia is pone of the most culturally diverse regions on our planet. There are many expressions of the people's faith which is dominated by the 'big 3" . . . Islam, Judaism and Christianity. It can at times be a very tumultuous area due to these differences.

This vast area is a resource rich area with its oil reserves, gold and so much more. At some time in the past, party of this region now designated as Southeast Asia was actually considered to be a part of the African continent . . . . but politics ultimately had their way with the redrawing of lines to suit its purposes. There is no 1 particular heritage one could attribute to this region of our world, for it appears to be more of a melting pot of many cultures who have passed through the regions due to trade, migration, religious, political and otherwise. For more information, please visit the following link.

https://en.wikipedia.org/wiki/Western_Asia

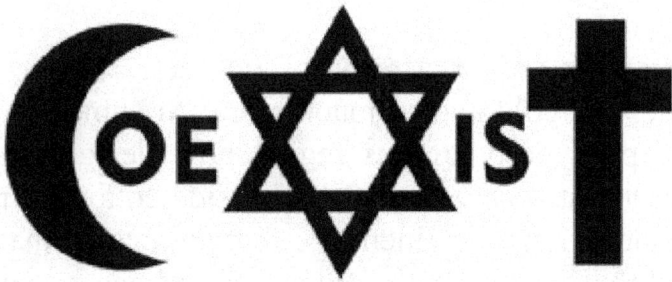

COEXISTENCE

Poets . . .
sowing seeds in the
Conscious Garden of Life,
that those who have yet to come
may enjoy the Flowers.

Poets, Writers . . . know that we are the enchanting magicians that nourishes the seeds of dreams and thoughts . . . it is our words that entice the hearts and minds of others to believe there is something grand about the possibilities that life has to offer and our words tease it forth into action . . . for you are the Poet, the Writer to whom the Gift of Words has been entrusted . . .

~ wsp

Poetry succeeds where instruction fails.

~ wsp

I Fly

because ... said the Dreamer to the world. I Can

www.iamjustbill.com

Gail Weston Shazor

Gail Weston Shazor

This is a creative promise ~ my pen will speak to and for the world. Enamored with letters and respectful of their power, I have been writing for most of my life. A mother, daughter, sister and grandmother I give what I have been given, greatfilledly.

Author of . . .

"An Overstanding of an Imperfect Love"
&
Notes from the Blue Roof

Lies My Grandfathers Told Me

available at Inner Child Press.

www.facebook.com/gailwestonshazor
www.innerchildpress.com/gail-weston-shazor
navypoet1@gmail.com

SiStars

I had always been told
That you too had been abandoned
Deep in the jungle
I wonder about your green canopied life
And I wonder if you wonder
About my green oak tree one
Lining the gravel road
In this deep forest of forgottenness

Our mothers could be twins
Separated at birth by Sam
That unforgiving uncle
Who found just one more reason
To be divisive
In our family, connected
His son, no more than a pawn
Without a reason save greed

He sent him to the bosom of
The Philippines
Japan
Korea
Vietnam
To seek the solace from the horror
From which he knew marked
His evermore

Where are you, my sister?
Now that we no longer bear
The pressure of uncle's need
To keep us separated…

4

Portals

We have forgotten the how of things
You and i
And it is only recently
That we can't find our way
I hold your hand in the dark
And we wander
Like this
Hands clasped tight to miss falls
And sometimes we forget
The what of things also
Glasses become slippers
And windows,
Maybe a fork in the road
Of memory
To sit and wait
On things to return to us
Or for them to be divinely revealed
In the cast of moonlight
I offer a blanket and
A cup of tea
To replace that which we search for
That is not found
Tonight
Or last night
But we hold out hope for tomorrow
For the finding
So that you may rest better and sooner
I watch you breathe
So shallow rise and fall
But I must be sure that you are
For that is what
I wait for
Every night

And I take note of the time
In a diary to capture the things shared
For the days grow long
As the memories disappear
The silences more pronounced
As you ponder silently
The times gone
And you forget to share them
With me
I read quietly all that I have missed
Of your life
Cementing them in my dreams
Of unspoiled landscapes
And colors
All the while noticing that
My hands have become yours
I revel in their working
Of needle and thread
Yarn and
Flour
And my memory is
Your hand
Guiding mine
I know that I may soon pass
Into the loss
And my daughter and I
Will take to
Walking
The night
For the forgotten things.

The measure of a woman…

What's the measure of a woman
Is it the way we move
To unheard music
Or carry the pain of indifference
Under our skin
Can you add weight to
My fingertips
To make me more sorrowful
Or even hold me to
A standard that you cannot
Bear the wanting of
Are my feelings not valid
In the day to day moments
Of the reconciliation of
Intentional hurts by others
That you view as histrionics
And thus the measure of wanting
Sits squarely on my shoulders
Should I bite my tongue
Is my waist too wide
Or my shoulders too broad
And how do you measure
The pressure of a spine
Bent under hateful words
Mitigated by the humor
And gentleness required
To hold your hand when
You need it
Some folks say we should
Be this smart
So I can fly to the moon
And still make cornbread
On the way back down

Fallen
Short
Where is the hope written
In the stars
That you would love me
Just because I am worthy
And not measured against
Another ideal of what is
Attractive
Why is the measure
Of a woman
Why is my measure
As a woman
And please tell me
Where I fall short
Of being beautiful and desired
What is the measure of a woman
And will you let the Maker know
Of his latest failure
So that I can
Be born again

Alicja Maria Kuberska

.

Alicja Maria Kuberska – awarded Polish poetess, novelist, journalist, editor. She was born in 1960, in Świebodzin, Poland. She now lives in Inowrocław, Poland.

In 2011 she published her first volume of poems entitled: "The Glass Reality". Her second volume "Analysis of Feelings", was published in 2012. The third collection "Moments" was published in English in 2014, both in Poland and in the USA. In 2014, she also published the novel - "Virtual roses" and volume of poems "On the border of dream". Next year her volume entitled "Girl in the Mirror" was published in the UK and "Love me" , " (Not)my poem" in the USA. In 2015 she also edited anthology entitled "The Other Side of the Screen".

In 2016 she edited two volumes: "Taste of Love" (USA), "Thief of Dreams" (Poland) and international anthology entitled " Love is like Air" (USA). In 2017 she published volume entitled "View from the window" (Poland). She also edits series of anthologies entitled "Metaphor of Contemporary" (Poland)

Her poems have been published in numerous anthologies and magazines in Poland, the USA, the UK, Albania, Belgium, Chile, Spain, Israel, Canada, India, Italy, Uzbekistan, Czech Republic, South Korea and Australia. She was a featured poet of New Mirage Journal (USA) in the summer of 2011.

Alicja Kuberska is a member of the Polish Writers Associations in Warsaw, Poland and IWA Bogdani, Albania. She is also a member of directors' board of Soflay Literature Foundation.

War in the Middle East

Memories like grains of sand,
during a storm in the desert,
swirled violently in the mind.
They hit hard, hurt badly.

Sight wanders around a desolate city.
I remember, there was a school there
and next to it a library and a flower shop.
The huge holes remained in the ground after them,
surrounded by the black stumps of the burnt trees.

Silence spills with a wide stream
through the empty streets and ashes.
It settles like dust on the broken glass.
Birds flew away, the absent inhabitants fell silent.
Sometimes the wind wails among the ruins
and then as the echo
the whistle of falling bombs comes back.

In a surviving building without a wall,
like on a great theatrical scene of life,
an old man is sitting alone and reading a book.
Hunger and fear have driven neighbors away.
He did not run away and became a guardian of hope.

Poor people suffer and die.
Politicians speak beautifully about peace,
about democracy and human rights.
Businessmen count the big profits
from the sale of weapons.

The vampires raise above the oil fields
to swab the last drop of black blood
from the tormented desert land.

Blue planet

I have this image of our beautiful planet in my mind.
This blue gem shines in the darkness of the universe.
It is a wonderful cradle of plants, animals, people
and was described as a paradise in the ancient stories.

I woke up terrified when this happy dream ended.
The green lungs of the Amazon have shrunk
and the world suffers from shortness of breath.
The vast ocean waters are covered with a thick layer of
plastic
and the genetically modified plants do not pour seeds onto
the soil.

I ask a man:
"Do you know what it will be tomorrow?
Did you forget who you are and where you come from?
Why did you recant your mother-Earth?"

You keep talking about money, profits, prosperity.
You draw the bars and worry about future incomes.
Instead of a dot at the end of your long lecture,
I saw one horrible word - *death*.

On the Border of Dream

I fell asleep.
And walked from reality to fantasy.
The subconscious put together a mosaic
Made from feelings, memories, dreams.

I do not know who I really am.
I float lightly upwards
To penetrate a glass blue sky.
I touch the black space during
My journey to distant galaxies.

Sudden anxiety and vision of the future
Bring me back to the Earth.
I fall down with crazy speed.

Your touch stopped and saved me.
We met in Eden, ate the prohibited apples.
Then you gave me your hand
And we soared together among the stars.

You whispered
That you were waiting for me a long time.
You said – "I love you"
Is this Chagall's painting,
Or just you and me?

I do not know how you entered.
My eyelids were closed.
Reality? Dream?

Jackie Davis Allen

Jackie Davis Allen

Jackie Davis Allen, otherwise known as Jacqueline D. Allen or Jackie Allen, grew up in the Cumberland Mountains of Appalachia. As the next eldest daughter of a coal miner father and a stay at home mother, she was the first in her family to attend and graduate from college. Her siblings, in their own right, are accomplished, though she is the only one, to date, that has discovered the gift of writing.

Graduating from Radford University, with a Bachelors of Science degree in Early Education, she taught in both public and private schools. For over a decade she taught private art classes to children both in her home and at a local Art and Framing Shop where she also sold her original soft sculptured Victorian dolls and original christening gowns.

She resides in northern Virginia with her husband, taking much needed get-aways to their mountain home near the Blue Ridge Mountains, a place that evokes memories of days spent growing up in the Appalachian Mountains.

A lover of hats, she has worn many. Following marriage to her college sweetheart, and as wife, mother, grandmother, teacher, tutor, artist, writer, poet and crafter, she is a lover of art and antiques, surrounding herself, always, with books, seeking to learn more.

In 2015 she authored *Looking for Rainbows, Poetry, Prose and Art*, and in 2017, *Dark Side of the Moon*. Both books of mostly narrative poetry were published by Inner Child Press and were edited by hulya n. yilmaz.

http://www.innerchildpress.com/jackie-davis-allen.php
jackiedavisallen.com

History, In The Making

Was it even plausible,
Conceivable, for a Chinese couple
To think of escape?
Of stowing away in a ship's belly?

Determined, two dreamed
Of hiding amongst trunks, baskets,
As part of the cargo, fleeing China.
And, the revolution.

Was it possible that this couple,
From Peking, highly educated,
Both with advanced degrees
Would succeed?

Or, that warmed, protected
By blanket's welcome
Of legality, they would
In fact, become USA citizens?

And, what were the odds
That we would become friends?
Or that, the political situation
Would change, in their favor?

Was it possible diplomatic relations
Would reawaken? Indeed, hands
On each side of the ocean, in 1972,
Threw open the doors!

A dream realized, to China,
They flew! Returning, however,
To their home in the USA. History was
In the midst of the making!

Carried back from Peking,
Thoughtfully, purchased and gifted
To me, most generously,
A treasured cloisonné vase.

Like a narrative poem,
They Chinese, I American,
We share and are
A part of each other's history.

We Are Offended

Oh, the fortitude
Of the minds
That make up the congress
Of a politico's cause.

Its seasons are indeterminate,
Yet admiration is conveyed
By the number of dollars and cents
With which votes are purchased.

It is an offensive position
That is recorded in history's ledger,
Where the brilliance
Of insight, of that which is right

Finds neither its persuasive image
In the mirror of truth,
But instead, finds itself defaced
By the media's meddling.

A New Day Is On Its Way!

Have you risen at the break of day,
Seen the sun rise between the sky scrapers,
The city streets slick and wet
               With the shadows of heels clicking?
               See how they meander here and there
               On the way to the day awaiting.

Over the air-ways, intelligence streaming,
A confusing combination of left, of right leanings,
Communistic Demagogs vs Constitutionalists.
               With considerable assertion, they
               Act as if they know it all. Always.
               They condemn those who believe differently.

Idealogues, dittoheads, so rude, they are charlatans,
A mob of xenophobes, it so appears, ones
Who advocate, support, criminal activity.
               Oh, most foul are they who incite violence.
               All the winsome faces are pleading. Even
               As hope climbs the rope to safety, it strengthens.

And of the plight of the meek, like a butterfly,
Some traditional ones have ceased to fight.
They seek only to live in peace.
               So too the plight of the worker bees.
               Are they waiting behind the trees,
               So as to erect a historical frieze?

Hang now a wreath of remembrance
To commemorate the demise of those
Who radically support illegality, dissidents.

Of probability's reason, do the zealots not
        Sit in the saddle of responsibility
Encumbered with a lack of common sense?

Let us overcome delusion's consequence
And unload the burden that contains the weight
Of the dismissive, the offensive socialists.
        Good morning America! Good morning!
          Have you not heard a new day is here?
It is time to turn away from the protagonists.

And marching to the band, with those whose
Rhythm calms the heart, pray that that faction casts
Down its recriminations and regrets.
        Step out in faith! In truth! Bravely accept
       That the best is yet to be. Choose now to reject
The demagogues and their propagandizing efforts.

Beware! Lest your demise arrive to seize
The spirit of your soul. Rise up, stand up!
Celebrate the revitalization of our nation.
        Seize the opportunity to enjoy participation
        In a new direction, a new season to breathe
         In the progress from a growing economy.

See how the grass is growing greener?
See how the branches of trees are reaching
Out to welcome all who cherish America?
        Happy are the citizens, no matter the color!
       They ring out and touch the soul of law abiders,
        With insight. With constitutional perspective.
Fill the air with a fragrance of loyalty,
One far beyond and away from hysteria's
Shrieks and the spurious shouts

Of the derisive, the divisive. Of course,
They serve as deterrents to those who see through
The fabrications of malcontents.

So, let us celebrate life and the day of recognition!
Let us jump for joy as we bask in the sunlight
Of a job well done. And, may we choose
To pocket colors green, silver and copper
For the day, when from discernment's
Commonsense, we raise our banners high.

Let us lift up our voices in unison, choosing
To ignore the clamor of those who
Would shout us down.
Let us stand on the truth, forging ahead!
Let us praise the Almighty.
A new day is here. More are on the way!

Jackie Davis Allen

Tzemin
Ition
Tsai

Dr. Tzemin Ition Tsai (蔡澤民博士) was born in Republic of China, in 1957. He holds a Ph.D. in Chemical Engineering and two Masters of Science in Applied Mathematics and Chemical Engineering. He is a professor at Asia University (Taiwan), editor of "Reading, Writing and Teaching" academic text. He also writes the long-term columns for Chinese Language Monthly in Taiwan.

He is a scholar with a wide range of expertise, while maintaining a common and positive interest in science, engineering and literature member.

He has won many national literary awards. His literary works have been anthologized and published in books, journals, and newspapers in more than 40 countries and have been translated into more than a dozen languages.

Psalms in Soldier's Arm

Footprints stampeded,
How many brother's bloods be stepped on?
Battle cries reached to the sky.
Attacking, Attacking, Shouting with the horn sounds.
The clouds were so deep.
The moon was so dark.
A single page can never write down completely.
How the bayonet was deeply scribed,
Psalms in Soldier's Arm.

Across the river in front,
Looking at the enemy stationed on the other side.
A fight imagery for the life-and-death
uprush and sudden well up in my heart.
Looking back,
I could saw the road has been covered up in the fog.
Why was I here,
my mind completely goes blank.

Besides on the first page,
it has been etched deeply the epitaphs of the soul.
The collection of poems left on the road,
were described those white rose petals belong to late
autumn here and there.
Sprinkling along the way,
those extremely tranquil seeds.
Never let
The psalms intoxicated in soldier's arm.

In My Dream, The Rainbow Never Sleep

Time passes
Try to maintain the same lengths of the grid
Such serenity does not contradict Einstein's cognition
A mountain edge touches the sunset
Cold in the red-hot
When the first light is covered
Driving the distant color clouds
Bringing down drizzle constantly
The light that penetrates the top corner of the window
Stretching at different angles of refraction
Arch bridge-like a rainbow
Call the colored dragon to ring
My window that never closed

Sitting on the dragon's dorsal fin
Tight scales protect me from pain
That silhouette soars up into the sky just like lightning
Just all of a sudden comes on the top of the rainbow
Smoothly
Such as Newton's ideal world can't find the friction
Only that fine silk clothing
Which
Makes every effort to shout in the air
In an attempt to prevent the falling down of the figure
With equal acceleration
To reach the terminal speed detached from the surface

When I fall in at the bottom of the clouds
Pray that gravitation will not forsake me
The quality is a very customary joke
Perhaps
Only let myself return to the dream again

Can no longer hear
Galileo's boast
Break through Aristotle's defense with wisdom
Where can I find?
The illusion of literature
Where to find scientific endorsement

That Clouds On Top Of The Valleys

Out of the window
The white layer upon layer
Are that clouds or fogs?
Causing waves of debate
That cup of tea old friends handed up
The cup is boiling hot and small
A burst of light white smoke
Did not cause anybody's attention
We two can only occupy the corner to feel ourselves
wronged, produce a forced smile

In this halfway up the mountain
Not high enough
Even the immortals are disdain to stay
That is the outside of the window
The wind rolled over and over again
Gone up
The people full of the house is only chasing out
All the cheers
Were kidnapped by the camera on the neck
In the panic, gradually away from
Gradually away from among the noisy

That corner
Even more lonely
We both look at each other to drink
Completely indifferent
That tea kettle
Has long been cooling
We found the answer in silence
Obviously
That the whole white vast out of the window
Are clouds but not
fogs

Tzemin Ition Tsai

Shareef
Abdur
Rasheed

Shareef Abdur Rasheed

Shareef Abdur-Rasheed, AKA Zakir Flo was born and raised in Brooklyn, New York. His education includes Brooklyn College, Suffolk County Community College and Makkah, Saudi Arabia. He is a Veteran of the Viet Nam era, where in 1969 he reverted to his now reverently embraced Islamic Faith. He is very active in the Islamic community and beyond with his teachings, activism and his humanity.

Shareef's spiritual expression comes through the persona of "Zakir Flo" . Zakir is Arabic for "To remind". Never silent, Shareef Abdur-Rasheed is always dropping science, love, consciousness and signs of the time in rhyme.

Shareef is the Patriarch of the Abdur-Rasheed Family with 9 Children (6 Sons and 3 Daughters) and 41 Grandchildren (24 Boys and 17 Girls).

For more information about Shareef, visit his personal FaceBook Page at :

https://www.facebook.com/shareef.abdurrasheed1
https://zakirflo.wordpress.com

Peace Piece

Middle East
where tormoil never cease
lands of righteous predecessors
from prophets(aws) who warned
to believers scorned
European crusaders came along
take Jerulsalam , their song
Adam, Ibrahim, Ismail, Isaq, Yaquob,
Lut, Shuayb, Yusef,Musa, Daoud,
Sulaiman, Yahya, Isa, Muhammad
peace and blessings be upon them all
gave the message all
" Only one(1) creator worthy of worship "
that's all
revealed Torah, Zaboor, Injeel, Qur'an
This was the lands they all walked upon
Sham, Syria, Egypt, Sini, Palestine ,
Turkey, Jordan, Arabia, Yemen, Lebanon
these were the lands revelation came
down upon
the books revealed for mankind to
stay upon
Middle East lands of the most sacred
Makkah, Madinah, Jerulsalam (Qutz)
but also beasts, evil never ceased
dem who come to cause mayhem, mischief
(fitnah) to destroy any semblance of peace
so much spirituality but also perpetual war
ever since between divine morals
and Shaitan's (Satan's) influence
immorality
to destroy the moral fiber of humanity

since time memorial until today it remains
the same way
where there's righteousness evil also exist
as a test to who will submit and uphold
or who will rebel and oppose
in this Middle East has been signs throughout
time and yet still more to come
look for the black flags of qurasoun
and Isa's (aws) return

food4thought = education

motherload
----
dem vie for whole pie
dem willing to die
in the try
dem live only for riches
dem sons of B!+ch$$$
never a day free of itchs
for whatever comes their
way with lots of digits
dem really dig it

motherload..,

the one that make dem
juices flow
nothing else matters yo
honesty, compassion ,
loyalty, humility got to go
all dem want is dough
can dem take it with them
when dem go
HELLS NO!
yet you can bet
that's the place
dem go
what a price to pay for
some dough
that won't be worth nothing
in the end friend, no mo

food4thought = education

X pectations
----

of wonderment
adornment embellished
by divine artistry
captivates me
for the sake of he
who created me
why do humans destroy
desecrate sacred ornaments?
adornment majestically
coordinated, orchestrated
not without purpose, benifit
enhance quality of life
so amazing disarms ability
to describe adequately
words fail to
so how can you?
yes this and more
cannot explain thus beyond
capacity of human brains
yet with all this incredible
beauty designed and delivered
flawlessly
mankind violates repeatedly,
lawlessly
although they benifit by that
which they destroy
even deny existence of he
who created all of it
including humanity?
explain this to me please
how it's all a accident

food4thought = education

Kimberly Burnham

Find yourself in the pattern. As a 28-year-old photographer, Kimberly Burnham appreciated beauty. Then an ophthalmologist diagnosed her with a genetic eye condition saying, "Consider life, if you become blind." She discovered a healing path with insight, magnificence, and vision. Today, 33 years later, a poet and neurosciences expert with a PhD in Integrative Medicine, Kimberly's life mission is to change the global face of brain health. Using health coaching, Reiki, Matrix Energetics, craniosacral therapy, acupressure, and energy medicine, she supports people in their healing from brain, nervous system, and chronic pain issues. As managing editor of Inner Child Magazine, Kimberly's 2019 project is peace, language, and visionary poetry with her recently published book, *Awakenings: Peace Dictionary, Language and the Mind, a Daily Brain Health Program.*

http://www.NerveWhisperer.Solutions
https://www.linkedin.com/in/kimberlyburnham

Stolen Peace Offering

There is a word in Balochi
spoken in Iran and Pakistan
makes me wonder what is mine
what is stolen
what kind of peace is sustained by an offering

"Muhnt" means a share
not all — only
a share of stolen property
restored to the owner
as a peace offering

And I wonder how often I am guilty
taking something
using it as if it is mine
not feeling enough
to give back a share

Of this earth I sense
do I take too much
give back enough
and when I do is it "muhnt"

Altic Roots of Sleeping Peaceful In Clean Air

Peace is a variation on "am"
to be quiet or sleep
in Tungus-Manchu
Mongolian and Turkic

In Proto Mongolian "amu" or "ami" takes on
rest peace and quiet
the Russian "мир" or "mir" means peace
but loses sleep

Descending from there
"amuxulaŋ" and "amara"
Mongolian peace
but also breathe easy
as if peace puts more oxygen into the air

In Kalmuck "amɣūləŋ" also breathe
and in Mogol "amūdu'i" is alive
as if deep sleep
gentle peace and clean air
are the stuff bringing us alive

Turkish Namaste

"Namaste" is peace
in Southern Zazaki spoken in Turkey
highlighting the people's Sanskrit roots

"Silam" similar to the Hebrew
"shalom" or Arabic "salam"
also means peace to these people of Turkey
an acknowledgement of Semitic influences

"Namaste" symbolic of green
spinning heart chakras
a divine light within the place
we can connect in peace with each other

I greet that place within you
which is love light and life
when I am in place and you are
we are not separate

I honor the place in you
where the entire universe resides
within me we are one
united

Elizabeth E. Castillo

Elizabeth Esguerra Castillo is a multi-awarded and an Internationally-Published Contemporary Author/Poet and a Professional Writer / Creative Writer / Feature Writer / Journalist / Travel Writer from the Philippines. She has 2 published books, "Seasons of Emotions" (UK) and "Inner Reflections of the Muse", (USA). Elizabeth is also a co-author to more than 60 international anthologies in the USA, Canada, UK, Romania, India. She is a Contributing Editor of Inner Child Magazine, USA and an Advisory Board Member of Reflection Magazine, an international literary magazine. She is a member of the American Authors Association (AAA) and PEN International.

Web links:

Facebook Fan Page

https://free.facebook.com/ElizabethEsguerraCastillo

Google Plus

https://plus.google.com/u/0/+ElizabethCastillo

Bedouins

Heirs of glory-
Nomadic people
of the Arabian desert
the sundry maladies
Taking flight into the night
Disparaged desert life
Savoring mem'ries of
aromatic wormwood
Bedouins-
Noble desert roamers
Enduring the unforgiving climate
From the vast wasteland
To the desert highway-
Dwelling in their beit a-sha'ar
Their constant wandering terhal
Taught them the value of hospitality
No matter how harsh desert life is
No traveller is turned away.

Zephyr

I am not of this world and I am evolving,
My soul is a spark in the Universe
Traveling in the speed of light years,
As I am ahead of my time.
A zephyr bringing a gentle touch
Summoning lost souls to ignite,
And light the amber
Rekindle the flame.
The enchanting echoes of the se,a
Calling forth fairies from the other world
Sprinkling pixie dusts to an ailing humanity
Bringing hope to wandering hearts.
The zephyr that I am brushes your cheeks each time,
Crooning sweet melodies, music that is so sublime
I am beyond your imagination taking you to oblivion.

Fragile

I have often seen innocent angels roaming the streets at
  night
Young vagabonds loitering dark alleys, scavengers
  searching for the light,
Tattered clothes, soiled feet, with eyes that question their
  mere existence
Young bloods, lost souls in need of careful attention and
  sustenance.

Fragile bodies crossing the roads, stopping cars to beg for
  money
Abandoned by some ruthless families, in the dark they hide
  their agony,
Some abused, maltreated by society who should be the first
  to care
Fallen angels seeking for the truth behind their helpless
  state.

Famish, greasy children pitifully sleeping on the cold
  pavement
It was not their choice to be born and suffer in such sad
  predicament,
Oh, God lay down your mercy on them and let them have
  the taste of life they were deprived
These precious one whom You adore, let your Light guide
  them and help them survive.

Joe Paire

Joe Paire

Joseph L Paire' aka Joe DaVerbal Minddancer . . .
is a quiet man, born in a time where civil liberties
were a walk on thin ice. He's been a victim of his
own shyness often sidelined in his own quest for
love. He became the observer, charting life's path.
Taking note of the why, people do what they do. His
writings oft times strike a cord with the
dormant strings of the reader. His pen the rosined
bow drawn across the mind. He comes full-frontal
or in the subtlest way, always expressing in a way
that stimulate the senses.

www.facebook.com/joe.minddancer

MENA

I want to explore your meaning
I want to export your resources
as voices from before imprint the sand
Jerusalem, Mecca with just a speck of Cairo
How often if ever,
have you traveled beyond your back door

I want to follow the foot path of belief
I want a dip in the red sea and pray to starry skies
Iraq, Iran, Saudi Arabia it's people
Live lives just like you or I how do you see them
Close your eyes
You'll hear the same laughter
The same cries for forgiveness
Humanity isn't on a map, it's how you live it

Page Filler

It was hot this day just not from the Sun
Fires from disenfranchised souls burned the flesh
We were all chard in this melting pot of humanity
All of a sudden we were the same
All of our differences went up in flames
Discussions turned into discussions
There was still home pride
There was still homefield advantage
The Planet had finally come together as one
Diversity came in it's true form
A dog was still a dog, it rained in the summer
Winter remained cold but Love
Man love; it went from fenced in borders
To love lived as it was written
Names had no more claim
Action was the thing
Who we are is what we do
A bad act could no longer be identified as a group
Music was judged by the sound, still true
But the few that chose color as a standard
Had no other choice except to accept
What was already commanded

Here We Are

What comes after a life filled with labor
Do you savor the days fishing
Or wishing you could turn back time
What are nest eggs and investments
Are you now confessing you never had a plan
I'm not talking stocks and 401k's
I'm talking about how you spend your days
Do you have time now with labor out of the way
Do you rise on reflex or rise with reflection
This life is more than a three day weekend
Receding hairlines thicker bellies
Here we are so tell me are the flowers more fragrant
Now that there's more time to smell them
Children, what will you tell them teach them
Is this the point where you finally meet them
If they're not already gone, was labor an excuse
A ruse an avoidance from parental employment
Or is it just what expected, pure enjoyment

hülya

n.

yılmaz

hülya n. yılmaz

A retired Liberal Arts professor, hülya n. yılmaz [sic] is Co-Chair and Director of Editing Services at Inner Child Press International, and a literary translator. Her poetry has been published in an excess of sixty anthologies of global endeavors. Two of her poems are permanently installed in *TelePoem Booth*, a nation-wide public art exhibition in the U.S. She has shared her work in Kosovo, Canada, Jordan and Tunisia. hülya has been honored with a 2018 WIN Award of British Colombia, Canada. She is presently working on three poetry books and a short-story collection. hülya finds it vital for everyone to understand a deeper sense of self and writes creatively to attain a comprehensive awareness for and development of our humanity.

hülya n. yılmaz, Ph.D.

Writing Web Site
hulyanyilmaz.com

Editing Web Site
hulyasfreelancing.com

Yemen

Oh, little angels of Yemen,
What is our world doing to you?

A "Human Rights Watch" has been out and about,
Traveling on our radar with ear-piercing cries for too long,
Trying to get our callous attention to listen to your plight,
Yet too many of us treat ourselves to a cowardly flight,
For that plane promises not to stop by any areas of conflict.
It will leave us intact inside and in peace forevermore
While we preserve our ever-so-precious comfort zone.

Thousands of you and your mothers, fathers,
Brothers, sisters, grandmothers, grandfathers,
Uncles, aunts, great uncles, great aunts
And undefined, unnamed guardians
Have been killed in less than a year.
6,872 butchered and 10,768 injured as of 2018.
"The actual civilian casualties are likely much higher",
Say many a source and add frightening numbers
As for those of you who have been displaced
Because of the fighting in your land. Not to
Neglect to mention how millions of you, not thousands . . .
Suffer from starvation and lack of survival care.

Oh, little angels of Yemen,
How grave your suffering must be!

The masterminds of the killing machines:
Saudi Arabia and the USA.
Should you survive the murdering fields . . .
Remember. Remember and write.
Next generations must know
How merciless we have been to you all.

not here

hearing the fireworks at Niagara Falls
thinking of war zones overcasting the globe
bombs, grenades, exterminated lives, blood,
much blood, unimaginable pain and utter fear
seeing is believing, says this language root
yet soul's eyes pierce the empirical
sees through and through
meets it all eye to eye
and takes it all in
loud and clear
there is so much suffering in open sight
that the mind freezes up,
crawls back to its womb
the heart is helpless
in its despair
and woes

Killing Our Children

A U.S. President of deservedly high honor
States his following insight of respected fame:
"We will not learn how to live together in peace
By killing each other's children."

Oh you, Honorable Mr. President,
Oh you, Honorable Jimmy Carter!
What is it that we are learning
In these indescribably dark times?
Why have we shamelessly forgotten
To feel responsible for our own shame?
We are killing our children by the thousands.
We are orphaning those who somehow survive.
Our dark history unavoidably will come back
To haunt us no matter how much we would want to revive
The "good ol' days" of the "good ol' US of A",
And before the rest of the world's eyes,
It will tear us apart piece by piece.

Unless . . . we begin to strive for peace
To abandon our cruelest ways, our fatal lies
And the murderous inventions we eagerly create
In order to kill the only innocent among us: our children . . .

Teresa E. Gallion

Teresa E. Gallion was born in Shreveport, Louisiana and moved to Illinois at the age of 15. She completed her undergraduate training at the University of Illinois Chicago and received her master's degree in Psychology from Bowling Green State University in Ohio. She retired from New Mexico state government in 2012.

She moved to New Mexico in 1987. While writing sporadically for many years, in 1998 she started reading her work in the local Albuquerque poetry community. She has been a featured reader at local coffee houses, bookstores, art galleries, museums, libraries, Outpost Performance Space, the Route 66 Festival in 2001 and the State of Oklahoma's Poetry Festival in Cheyenne, Oklahoma in 2004. She occasionally hosts an open mic.

Teresa's work is published in numerous Journals and anthologies. She has two CDs: *On the Wings of the Wind* and *Poems from Chasing Light*. She has published three books: *Walking Sacred Ground, Contemplation in the High Desert* and *Chasing Light*.

Chasing Light was a finalist in the 2013 New Mexico/Arizona Book Awards.

The surreal high desert landscape and her personal spiritual journey influence the writing of this Albuquerque poet. When she is not writing, she is committed to hiking the enchanted landscapes of New Mexico. You may preview her work at

http://bit.ly/1aIVPNq or *http://bit.ly/13IMLGh*

The Pink City

You are an ancient marvel that disappeared
for many centuries. Sheltering a history
as a major trade route filled with chaos,
wealth and beauty. You were exposed
to the world again in 1812.

Your reemergence led to distinguished titles:
World Heritage Site in 1985, one of the new
Seven Wonders of the World in 2007.
Sheltered in the remote desert mountains
of Jordan, you are the Country's treasure.

Your carved rose-red sandstone rock
facades, became even more known
around the world because of Indiana Jones.

As a heavily visited tourist attraction,
Homo Sapiens come from
all over planet earth to experience
your natural splendor and eloquence.
Will we love you to death Petra?

Fire Danger

Driving on the interstate
an exit and left turn
leads to a welcome sign:
Cibola National Forest.

Bright yellow reflects
high fire danger today.
A familiar sign in recent years.

The sky hordes its water blossoms.
Evergreens hang onto life.
Perseverance is a character
trait of the big trees.

The undergrowth waits
for the flames of nature
to use them to season the soil.

Sacred Howl

Out of the sea she howls
and it is heard all the way to the sky.
.

An Angel reaches and pulls her
to the clouds,

drops her on dry land amidst sculptures
impossible to define or describe.

Walk in the belly of the rock.
Feel the harmony of God's sacred paintings.

There is no need for words to explain
as understanding swims through the veins.

What a blessing to experience
the power of a sacred howl.

Ashok
K.
Bhargava

Ashok K. Bhargava

Ashok Bhargava is a poet, writer, community activist, public speaker, management consultant and a keen photographer. Based in Vancouver, he has published several collections of his poems: Riding the Tide, Mirror of Dreams, A Kernel of Truth, Skipping Stones, Half Open Door and Lost in the Morning Calm. His poetry has been published in various literary magazines and anthologies.

Ashok is a Poet Laureate and poet ambassador to Japan, Korea and India. He is founder of WIN: Writers International Network Canada. Its main objective is to inspire, encourage, promote and recognize writers of diverse genres, artists and community leaders. He has received many accolades including Nehru Humanitarian Award for his leadership of Writers International Network Canada, Poets without Borders Peace Award for his journeys across the globe to celebrate peace and to create alliances with poets, and Kalidasa Award for creative writings.

Sweet Salt

Looking out the window
joy persists
everything outside gives me a spark
a collaborative work
farmhands planting rice seedling
in the knee-deep water
the day is long.

The timelessness
serene beauty overflows
all along the highway
a blue sky and
stiff lipped trees
blinking at
infinity.

Only one thing
one distraction
what would be for dinner tonight?

Sour vinegar, hot chilies
or fish sauce
for the boiled rice?

Stepping out from the bus:
the salt
from sweat makes
the skin stick.
I love to ride A/C bus.

Typhoon Track

Trapped in the middle of nowhere
In a dark and soggy hut.

No choice except
to wait
out the typhoon.

All night at
a hesitant place
our bodies burn.

I become a wick
you the oil.

Carefully we
cup the flicker
whole night long.

We churn with
the raging typhoon
until the dawn
yields the nectar of life.

We leave, alone
as newly
awakened souls.

Haiku

1.
silvery mirror
shadows of my past
old house besides river Nile

2.
drips of rain
sound of temple bells
the spirit of childhood

3.
overwhelming imagination
crowds and pyramids
the ancient game of powerplay

4.
the sand dune gardens
buses shuttle the blues
busy like bees

5.
sun rises
the world we live in
blooms

Caroline
'Ceri Naz'
Nazareno

Carolin 'Ceri' Nazareno

Caroline Nazareno-Gabis a.k.a. Ceri Naz, born in Anda, Pangasinan known as a 'poet of peace and friendship', is a multi-awarded poet, journalist, editor, publicist, linguist, educator, and women's advocate.

Graduated cum laude with the degree of Bachelor of Elementary Education, specialized in General Science at Pangasinan State University. Ceri have been a voracious researcher in various arts, science and literature. She volunteered in Richmond Multicultural Concerns Society, TELUS World Science, Vancouver Art Gallery, and Vancouver Aquarium.

She was privileged to be chosen as one of the Directors of Writers Capital International Foundation (WCIF), Member of the Poetry Posse, one of the Board of Directors of Galaktika ATUNIS Magazine based in Albania; the World Poetry Canada and International Director to Philippines; Global Citizen's Initiatives Member, Association for Women's rights in Development (AWID) and Anacbanua. She has been a 4th Placer in World Union of Poets Poetry Prize 2016, Writers International Network-Canada ''Amazing Poet 2015'', The Frang Bardhi Literary Prize 2014 (Albania), the sair-gazeteci or Poet-Journalist Award 2014 (Tuzla, Istanbul, Turkey) and World Poetry Empowered Poet 2013 (Vancouver, Canada).

geographic brain

we both explored
the land, the water and the air
of our breathing tanks;
as we embrace differences
we are both webbing history
from here to your place,

we both exist
in the terrestrial circuits
of our body fluids,
up and down, or circling
 in gravitational laments
and poetic climes

we revolt in wilderness
like thunder and storm
time after time, we popple
in the landscape of memories

the miracle that we are

you become the voice
in a spun of moment
the scene of infected vibe
to a soul belter.

you come in my mind,
exquisite lush of green,
your charm send me
nature, revival, and peace.

you are present in the dew drops
when my mind is drenched
in the miracle of seconds.

now hold my hand,
as we count the numberless stars
we shine together,
every time our eyes meet.

Rise and believe

you are more than mapping gates
of possibilities,
spawning on the globe's eyes,
sifted by time and pressure,
you become pearls,
in the wide ocean
of wonders.
as i stretch my arms
to reach you,
unzip the warring spheres
of shadows and luminescence,
i frequently speak
to vermilion stars,
that i rise to believe
in greatness.

Swapna Behera

Swapna Behera is a bilingual contemporary poet, author, translator and editor from Odisha, India .She was a teacher from 1984 to 2015 . Her stories, poems and articles are widely published in National and International journals, and ezines, and are translated into different national and International languages. She has penned four books. She was conferred upon the Prestigious International Poesis Award of Honor at the 2nd Bharat Award for Literature as Jury in 2015, The Enchanting Muse Award in India World Poetree Festival 2017, World Icon of Peace Award in 2017, and the Pentasi B World Fellow Poet in 2017.. She is the recipient of Gold Cross Of Wisdom Award ,the medal for The Best Teachers of the World from World Union of Poets in 2018, and The LIfe time Achievement Award ,The Best Planner Award, The Sahitya Shiromani Award, ATAL BiHARI BAJPAYEE AWARD 2018, Ambassador De Literature Award 2018 .She is the Ambassador of Humanity by Hafrikan Prince Art World Africa 2018 and an official member of World Nation's Writers Union ,Kazakhstan2018. At present she is the manager at Large, Planner and Columnist of The Literati, the administrator of several poetic groups ,the member of the Special Council of Five of World Union of Poets and the Cultural Ambassador of Inner Child Press U.S.

The Saga of Konark....

the majestic spine of time
the paramount temple
on the shore of Chandrabhaga
peeping to the arcane sky
the fostered skill of twelve hundred artisans
ardent magic of their lost youth and visions
the fragrant perfume of their sweats,
salty tears of their wives
transferred stones into an epic
the liberated soulful cadence
the euphoria of their bloody fingers
Aah! their stooping bones
their onerous fingers beating the anvils
the crinkles on their faces
sublime structures
images on the stones
the mammoth monolithic structures
of elephant men, lion or erotica
the oscillating eye pupils of those artists
like the pendulum of time
somewhere whispers
the vintage history
the aftermath of long twelve years
the poking passions
fiery fire of their damsels, their oily hair
far off in the villages garlanding
the cuddles of nights
murmuring water
witnessing the miracle
the provoking psychic
flickering primeval
heartbeats synchronising anvils
condense the abstract mystic figures

thou art glued on the wheel of time
rain and wintry sleepless nights
the twelve stone wheels
pulled by seven horses
Oh ! the monarch of time
the epitome of Kalinga architecture
humbly bent towards the East
to receive the first sun ray of the dawn

the profiles of Sun promises;
the healer of all impurities
the proximity of promises
the tinkling tricks
made you so grandeur
the dazzling saffron Sun
the blisters axiom
singing the saga of time
in the horizon

as a conjuror stands the Konark ;
the scathe penetrates the soul
astounding odyssey of time
dances the Black Pagoda,
the luminous
reflection of all time zones
the aura of episodes on the sand ....

note :
Chandrabhaga is the name of a river
Konark is the Sun Temple of Odisha in India
Kalinga is the ancient name of Odisha state in India

The Figure of A Pagan

his eclipsed aura
above
the horizon
or
behind him
on
the debris
or
on the flowers

his rhymes sustain
in
aftermath
engraved in words
his outline is reborn
on
every traffic square

he speaks in silence
writes the unseen
his blood sparkles in dark

HE is a
pagan
the voice ....

The Last Smoke Of A Chimney

here hangs the clothes on the strings
there lies the basket of eggs
  the hen sitting on it
was cooked by the soldiers
long before

the kitchen is smoke free
the corn fields burnt
the girls raped;
pregnant teenaged girls
 carrying unknown faces,
unspoken bruises in their nipples
seized their lips

the granny looks at the sky
for the first shower of smoke free sky
her ears alert
not to get the sound of the land mine explosions
the land became holes
the last song of a wounded soldier echoes
the country is only a boundary in the hearts
but can the smoke have any border line

each kitchen chimney speaks love
may it be in any refugee tent
or in a kurdish village
or in yezidi schools
each child needs love and care
each Malala needs a school and not a bullet
each woman needs dignity
each refugee camp needs water and food

the last smoke of a kitchen chimney
bleeds and cries
 for the first cease fire of any ethnic wars
coz each migration is so painful
may it be for life or in death .....

Malala Yousafzai , is the recipient of 2014 Nobel Peace
Prize at the age of 17 who stayed in theSwat valley in
Khyber , North West of Pakistan .She was shot by the
Talibans but she survived .She is the human right activist .
Kurdish are the ethnic groups of people of Kurdistan
Yazidi are ethnic groups of people of Northern Iraq

Albert
'Infinite'
Carrasco

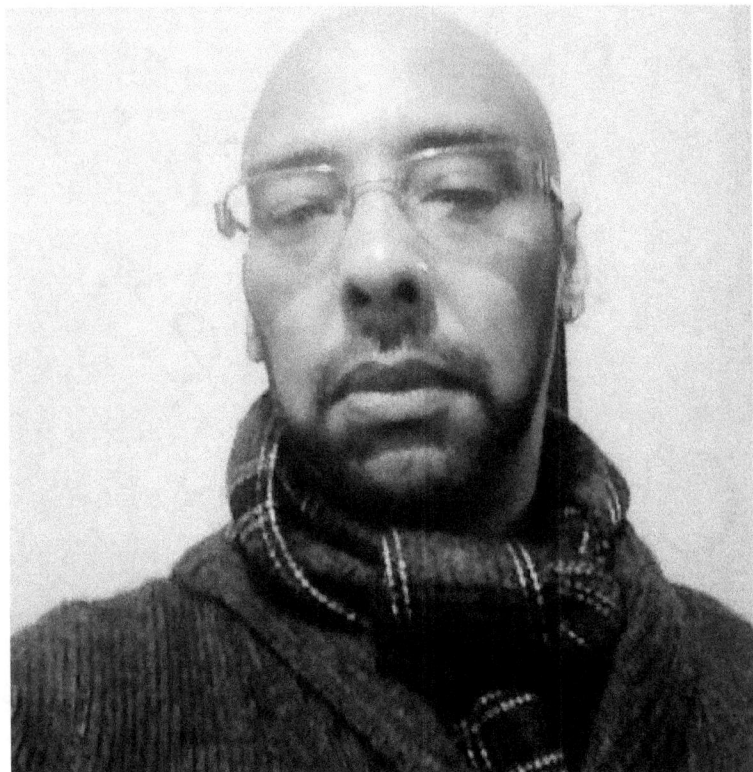

I'm a project life philanthropist, I speak about the non ethical treatment of poor ghetto people. Why? My family was their equal, my great grandmother and great grandfather was poor, my grandmother and grandfather, my mother and father, poverty to my family was a sequel, a traditional Inheritance of the subliminal. I paid attention to the decades of regression, i tried to make change, but when I came to the fork in the road and looked at the signs that read wrong < > right, I chose the left, the wrong direction, because of street life interactions a lot around me met death or incarceration. I failed myself and others. I regret my decisions, I can't reincarnate dead men, but I can give written visions in laymens. I'm back at that fork in the road, instead of it saying wrong or right, I changed it, now it says dead men < > life.

Infinite poetry @lulu.com

Alcarrasco2 on YouTube

Infinite the poet on reverbnation

Infinite Poetry

http://www.lulu.com/us/en/shop/al-infinite-carrasco/infinite-poetry/paperback/product-21040240.html

The Middle East

18 countries, 60 languages.
Many religions temples and parishes.
As-salamu alaikum
Wa alaikum assalaam
peace be with you.
And upon you be peace.
That's an Arabic Islamic greeting,
In the Middle East.
Sand surrounding pyramids in Egypt,
Skyscrapers pierce the sky in Dubai,
The great mosque of mecca in Saudi Arabia,
The Cairo Citadel are just a few of many beautiful visuals.
Some travel through deserts on camels,
Some drive through cities in expensive cars
and pets, they own exotic animals.

Manifestation

Infinite's a urban poetic titan, I lived what's written and spoken. My rhymes derived from poverty and from being on the frontline of white crime to end hard times. I can tell you how it is to be broke, how to cook, stretch, chop and shave coke, how easy it is to lose your life when you see death approaching and you choke, how hard it is to cope living without a homie after gun smoke and how it feels to have stacks on stacks, jewels and low pros under a shinny coat. I'm from the Bronx, the east part, Castle Hill, the big park, projects, shooters, hustlers, fiends and c-ciphers, that's trap art. When I'm on stage you're looking at and hearing a legend in his prime, a veteran of the boy and girl grind, a survivor... I fought hard to make sure the monitor attached to me didn't flatline after getting hit two times. I'm not looking for fame, everybody knows me, I'm not looking to be under the lime light, I appreciate my privacy so I stay low key.

I came to share my eye sores, because what my eyes saw will open minds more, I've seen it all before, I've seen em ball, I've seen em fall, get placed in the floor and a lifetime of dining in a chow hall. My bars are manifestations of my visions.

Results

I rolled with boss nikkas as we built home base, I understood that when shit got established some will want to franchise and run their own place. The entire team had the same dream, I know because we shared them chasing cream. We was in the trenches on the park benches imagining ourselves living in cribs with a few acres surrounded by gates or fences. We was hustling hard, 365 days a year no days off unless we was locked up, on the run or recouping from gettn shot up. The grind took all our time. Everything was done as a unit, all the PC went into one pot, we lived by the phrase... we all we got. From boys to men, we grew. From rags to riches, we blew. Everybody is dip, necks and wrist dripped, stood with something foreign and stick, riddn shotty was something thick. We done came up in the bricks. Life was good great.

It would've stood that way but some wanted their own block and color of purée, I knew the outcome of that from watching the OG's play, I explained that it'll be best to stay but I didn't want to stand in their dreams way, no matter what I had their back, Vayas con dios like gangsters say, the end result was always bars or death from gun play.

.

Eliza Segiet

After earning a Master's Degree in Philosophy at the Jagiellonian University in Krakaw, Poland, Eliza Segiet proceeded with her post-graduate studies in the fields of Cultural Knowledge, Penal Revenue and Economic Criminal Law, Arts and Literature and Film and Television Production in the Polish city, Lodz.

With specific regard to her creative writings, the author describes herself as being torn in her passion for engaging in two literary genres: Poetry and Drama. A similar dichotomy from within is reflected on Segiet's own words about her true nature: She likes to look at the clouds, but she keeps both of her feet set firmly on the ground.

The author describes her worldview as being in harmony with that of Arthur Schopenhauer: "Ordinary people merely think how they shall 'spend' their time; a man of talent tries to 'use' it".

Canyon

Locked in centuries ago
rock marks:
feet, chamois, camel...
soundlessly shout:
– the human left a trail.
There was,
is and will be
the one
who will go down in history –
for some
a thinking human,
because they drew,

for others
a mindless vandal,
because they destroyed.

Locked in centuries ago
rock marks
soundlessly shout:

– do not help erosion.
Everything will pass on its own.

translated by Artur Komoter

Incomplete

In the rocky window
they were enfolded
by the wind.
The Martian landscape
of the galactic desert,
sun-scorched sand -
will be a remembering.

Filled with an echo
of multi-colored rocks,
they are more aware

– to live
one does not need much.

Surrounded by artifacts
– without memories we will be
incomplete.

translated by Artur Komoter

Odorless Roses

Between odorless roses,
with an always silent friend,
in the smell of the desert
the Bedouin goes.
Under the umbrella of the sky
is the other one.
When the sun becomes a memory –
it drifts away.
Close, yet distant
in the morning they find already
the silent unity of gestures.

translated by Artur Komoter

William
S.
Peters Sr.

Bill's writing career spans a period of over 50 years. Being first Published in 1972, Bill has since went on to Author in excess of 40 additional Volumes of Poetry, Short Stories, etc., expressing his thoughts on matters of the Heart, Spirit, Consciousness and Humanity. His primary focus is that of Love, Peace and Understanding!

Bill says . . .

I have always likened Life to that of a Garden. So, for me, Life is simply about the Seeds we Sow and Nourish. All things we "Think and Do", will "Be" Cause and eventually manifest itself to being an "Effect" within our own personal "Existences" and "Experiences" . . . whether it be Fruit, Flowers, Weeds or Barren Landscapes! Bill highly regards the Fruits of his Labor and wishes that everyone would thus go on to plant "Lovely" Seeds on "Good Ground" in their own Gardens of Life!

to connect with Bill, he is all things Inner Child

www.iaminnerchild.com

Personal Web Site

www.iamjustbill.com

SWA

In a land of many
Where many have traversed,
Many have traded,
Many have settled
And raised families,
Generations, cities
And farms

We have built communities
Developed our individual cultures
And worshipped at different altars

Our soil is rich
And sparse,
Alive
And dormant,
But not dead!
We have sands and forests,
Rivers and Seas,
And ships sailing
And in waiting . . .
We speak a multitude of tongue

They call us Southwest Asia now
As the lines are constantly being drawn . . .

Yes, we have politics too, but we do not attempt
To control the world,
But we do have our
Influences

SWA = South West Asia

Born Free

It was July 4th, 1957
When you came out
To play with the world
Giving of,
Sharing,
Your graceful ways

You toiled,
Migrated,
Mitigated
Through its spoiled ways

Your days were numbered,
Somehow I believed
You knew this,
But that did not stop you
From nurturing
With love
The seed you were given

The living ones
You left behind
Still linger so,
But you knew,
And still know
That there is still
Much work to be done

Your sons
And your daughters
Still struggle
To draw their due quarter

From the lessons of heart
You left behind,
Though it has now been
13 years and 2 days
Since you crossed that line
Into the heavenly realm

You are free, yes,
But we are still enslaved
To some degree
To that memory of you,
Amongst other things,
Though, like you,
We too were
Born Free.

Dedicated to
Virisa Anne Cohen-Peters
4 July 1957 ~ 2 July 2006

Is enough

Do you love me ...
Enough,
Enough to accept me as I am?

Do you love me enough
To discard your preferences,
Longing and wistful definitions
Expectations and demands
That I meet your approval?

Do you love me enough
To embrace my
Idiosyncratic behaviours,
My eccentricities,
My eclecticism,
My oddities,
My uniqueness,
And my charm?

Do you love me enough
To forgive my ignorance,
My indifference,
My lethargy,
My interests,
My habits,
My humanity?

Do you love me enough
To hold me
When I hurt,
Even though
I am the source of my pain?
Do you love me enough

Do you love me enough
To see that
I love you
Through it all,
The awkwardness,
The ambivalence,
The detachment,
The space between us?

Do you love me enough,
Do you love your self enough,
Do we love each other enough
To see that light
Within us,
Between us,
Bathing our 'I am-ness'
With the possibilities
Of what we can become
If we but let go
And love enough

Enough ...
I am 'enough' ...
Are you?

August
2019
Featured Poets

~ * ~

Shola Balogun

Bharati Nayak

Monalisa Dash Dwibedy

Mbizo Chirasha

I Fly

because ... said the Dreamer to the world. I Can

Shola
Balogun

Shola Balogun, poet, playwright and filmmaker has been featured as a guest writer and contributor, especially in the areas of poetry, postcolonial studies and dramatic criticism to various magazines, anthologies and journals. He studied Theatre Arts at the University of Ibadan. Balogun lives in Lagos, Nigeria

Earth Poem

Wine for your thoughts.

Raft of corn seeds,
Whispers in the attic,
The locked eyes in the helve,
The treading of the sole of the foot
In the winepress. You heard tell
That trampling tongues
Birth Belial roots
In the dark pool of rushes?

Child, meddle not with the shadows.
Stones tasted wine in time past.

You Must Pledge A Grinding Stone to Kernels

It was nobler to forestall the dawn.

Darkfall scantily clad in a stirring wooden mask,
The proletariate of silence spiteful,
Languid to approaching lingerers.

Is it with dry morsels of bean cake and forsaken corn
You shall often speed to the standing- place
of the spirit?

Not unless the ministrant forebear wine,
Softening bud and tenderer nuts.

Such petulant panic of a measured temper
Is native taste to peasant-hour.

Tiresias

Now my tongue is chiseled with riddles.

I have seen several severe dances
Saved for the last brawl,
Of fouled rumps rumbling
To the beats of bayonets
And the witless witness
Seeking solace in the stunts
Of jabbering jury.

I have seen the insidious fury
Of the greedy gods,
Their garrulous garbadines
And the mirthless mimicry
Of deluded sickly siblings
Yearning to mete eternity
With the cistern of loaded rifles:

I have heard the thrilling rancour
Of strutting sycophants,
The longings of zealous zealots
And the feline concerto
Of hostile histrionics caressing
The jugular of barren seers.

Tiresias!

There is *tiro in my eyes.
I have come to chronicle
The well-made malaise
Of marionettes in the land.

*tiro: Eye salve

Bharati Nayak

Bharati Nayak, born in the year 1962 ,is a bilingual poet, critique and translator from Odisha, an Indian State lying on its eastern coast. She writes in English and Odia. Her poems have been published in many magazines, journals, anthologies and e-books of national and international repute such as *Rock Pebbles, Orissa Review, Utkal Prasang, Creation and Criticism, Circular Whispers, Nova Literature-Poesis, Poetry Against Terror, 56 Female Voices of Poetry, The Four Seasons Poetry Concerto, Tunes From the Subcontinent, Amaravati Poetic Prism, Bhubaneswar Review* and the like.

She has published three poetry books-
1-*Padma Paada* (A poetry book in Odia language)
2-*Words Are Such Perfect Traitors*
3-*A Day for Myself*

Bharati Nayak

A   Cracked   Letter

I chanced to see the letters,
You wrote me a long long ago,
Each alphabet,
Stood before me with an image,
That hid so many stories, and
So many tender moments of affection.

I held them in my palm,
Smelt the scent,
That was hidden under each syllable.
The letters were worn out by time,
The folds cracked,
As each one of them was read and re-read
Innumerable times,
Lost the strength
To bear the emotions
That were falling heavy on them.
Some syllables had vanished by tear drops,
Some had vanished in the folds.

As I held the letter,
Bits of paper fell in my lap,
Reminding me of the time gap.
I gathered the torn pieces
Tried to join them in their places
But some syllables were
Never to be found.

Our Dear Parrot

You stayed with me as a fond memory.
The green feathers and your chattering.
I know you were angry when we pulled your tail
and tormented you inside the cage.
But you were our mother's pet.
and you loved to be fed
with rice and milk by her hands.
The cage was shut from outside,
But you could easily open it from inside,
and enjoy the pleasure of freedom at your own will.

Like a child you loved my mother,
showed your emotions,
by spreading your wings and pecking,
at her fingers,
giving her,
bits of your own food.

It was pleasure to observe,
the tenderness besotted with love.
You were part of our family,
Loved and cared,
But one day you flew away.

Perhaps you wanted to discover,
A world outside the cage,
You did not come back,
Perhaps you did not know,
How to return.
Perhaps you did not know,
And would never know,
We were crying,
Mother and we,
Waiting.

Words Are Such Perfect Traitors

They rise in me
Like large waves
Overpowering me
I surrender to them
I feel so powerless.

They are beautiful
Colorful
Dreams floating across sky
Like a milky way
I just want to hold them
In my hand
Oh my hand, so small to hold.
They slip away
I love
To enclose them
In a bracket of words
But-
Words are such perfect traitors- - -

Monalisa
Dash
Dwibedy

Monalisa Dash Dwibedy is an IT Consultant by day and a writer by night. A bilingual writer, her English poems were published in many international anthologies and magazines. She is the author of Odia poetry book "Anjulae Smruti" (A handful of memory). She loves travelling and feels mountains call her when she is nearby. She aspires to befriend the Himalayan mountain ranges and wishes she could talk to the Sun and the Moon someday. Monalisa lives in Toronto, Canada.

She can be reached at **Monalisa.dash@gmail.com**

The New Immigrant

Where are you from?
You ask.
I am from the land of
Wealth and misery,
The mystic range of
Himalayan Mountains.
Land of bomb blasts, surgical strikes and sufferings,
Land of love, yoga, sun and devotion,
I am from a border village of India and Pakistan.

How many of your villagers have come here?
You ask.
They are few, alive with their past misfortunes,
Holding onto their indescribable emotions,
They still fear a stranger, like an unknown enemy,
Taking one day at a time,
Grabbing every little happiness,
You will know when you see them.
That terrifying brightness in their eyes,
Tells about their life near the border of death,
They lived and died at the same time, many times,
A circle of infinite tiredness in their face,
The way they laugh, you can envision their whole life in
that laughter.
No one can laugh like them.

This is a very new city, Do you feel home?
You ask.
On the hillside in the bright daylight,
I see the birds fly with same zeal in their flight,
On the grass near that lawn,
I watch the new plants being born, the same way they are

born on my land.
When it rains here,
Leafs shine.
Hungry soil soaks the first rain like a sponge.
The smell of the rain-hit earth,
The smell of home.
This summer, your city with blue-white skies,
High-rise buildings,
Tulips in the spring and Mary-golds in winter
Felt like home.

You really did not love me

The day death sent a message,
After taking away the life of my husband,
An army major.
A warrior gave all he could,
Returned home, wrapped in the tricolor.
"That's the life of a soldier,
He told me in our first night.
A pain so deep, so devastating,
Broke my heart into millions pieces,
I sat alone in dark despair,
Shedding silent tears.
My dear mother, when you told me to smash
All my bangles on the tenth day of his death,
I thought you really did not love me.

The basket of grief and sorrow,
So heavy to carry,
I was unable to cross the road of life, alone.
When I wanted a shoulder to lean on,
Heal my spirit,
My dear father, when you told me
Thinking marriage for a widow is sin,
I thought, you really did not love me.

Every morning I put a fake mask,
The mask makes everything seem all right,
No one knows I cry every night, all night.
The nightmares just won't go away.
When all I needed was a hand to hold on,
To start life all over again,
My dear friend, when you did not invite me

To your brother's marriage, thinking I may bring
misfortune to your family as a widow,
I for sure knew, you were never my friend.

I am still the same human being.
Just like any of you.
When I had no role to play in the death of my loved one
Why am I punished?

I want to live my life
I am the urge to move beyond my past.
I am hope.
I am the beginning of each new day.

Soul of a Forest

Night did not have a death wish, but
When dawn started its rhythmic dance
Night was willing to die for the day.
I took my heart for a walk in the forest
Moon was still on the sky,
Not suffocated with the arrival of the Sun,
Soon, the Sun shined through the dense trees
I jogged listening to the magic whisper of the wind,
Blowing on my face, caressing my tresses.
On the banks of a nameless river,
With the fragrance of wild jasmines,
With the songs of earthworms, peacocks,
I chorused, singing the song of life.
My spirit danced with the wind,
I giggled like a girl,
On my return from my morning walk,
I knew the forest had a soul.

Mbizo
Chirasha

© Mgcini Nyoni

Mbizo Chirasha is a Literary Arts Projects Curator, Art Activism Catalyst, an Internationally anthologized Poet, a Writer in Residence, a Word Press Blogs Publisher and Social Media Publicist. Mbizo Chirasha is the Originator/Instigator of the Zimbabwe We Want Poetry Campaign

http://tuckmagazine.com/tag/mbizo-chirasha/Zimbabwe

We Want Poetry Campaign /Mbizo Chirasha, http://www.newzimbabwe.com/showbiz-39824-Poems+on+Zim+abuses+to+be+read+in+the+US/show biz.aspx,

www.facebook.com/100thousandpoetsforpeace-zimbabwe

www.acaciabookstore.com/home/24-inside-disgrace-land.

KONGO

Your past is a mint of blood and tears

Daughters Mbizo Chirasha is a Literary Arts Projects

Curator, Art tearing their way to decay

Sons castrated by poverty and superguns,

Kongo, a dream battered and bruised

Your conscience poliorised by oppressive -dans

Highways clogged with hatred and vendetta

Gutters donating stench and typhoid

Kongo, let my poetry feed your withering dreams for

guns, insult the tired memories

Of voters.

Children Of Xenophobia

Children eating bullets and firecrackers

Beggars of smile and laughter

Silent corpses sleeping away fertile dreams

Povo chanting new nude wretched slogans

Overstayed exiles eating beetroot and African potato

Abortions and condoms batteries charging the lives of

nannies and maids

Children of barefoot afternoons and uncondomized

nights

Sweat chiseling the rock of your endurance

The heart of Soweto, Harare, Darfur, Bamako still

beating like drums

Violence fumigating peace from this earth.

Diary Of Povo

Another whistle from election fervent fathers

Another ululation from slogan drugged mothers

In chimoio we roasted bullets like mealie cobs for

breakfast

In nyadzonia we boiled grenades like cassava for lunch

meals

In magagao we munched parcel bombs like tropical

fruit

In gorongoza, we learnt totems of war and syndromes

of propaganda

Today, our ears are deaf with sediments of slogans

We are the povo

Remembering

our fallen soldiers of verse

Janet Perkins Caldwell

February 14, 1959 ~ September 20, 2016

Alan W. Jankowski

16 March 1961 ~ 10 March 2017

Coming
April 2020

The
World Healing, World Peace
International Poetry Symposium

Stay Tuned

for more information
intouch@innerchildpress.com
'building bridges of cultural understanding'
www.innerchildpress.com

Inner Child Press

News

Poetry Posse Members

We are so excited to share and announce a few of the current books, as well as the new and upcoming books of some of our Poetry Posse authors.

On the following pages we present to you ...

Jackie Davis Allen

Gail Weston Shazor

hülya n. yılmaz

Nizar Sartawi

Faleeha Hassan

Fahredin Shehu

Caroline 'Ceri' Nazareno

Eliza Segiet

William S. Peters, Sr.

Now Available at
www.innerchildpress.com

No Illusions

Through the Looking Glass

Jackie Davis Allen

Now Available at

www.innerchildpress.com

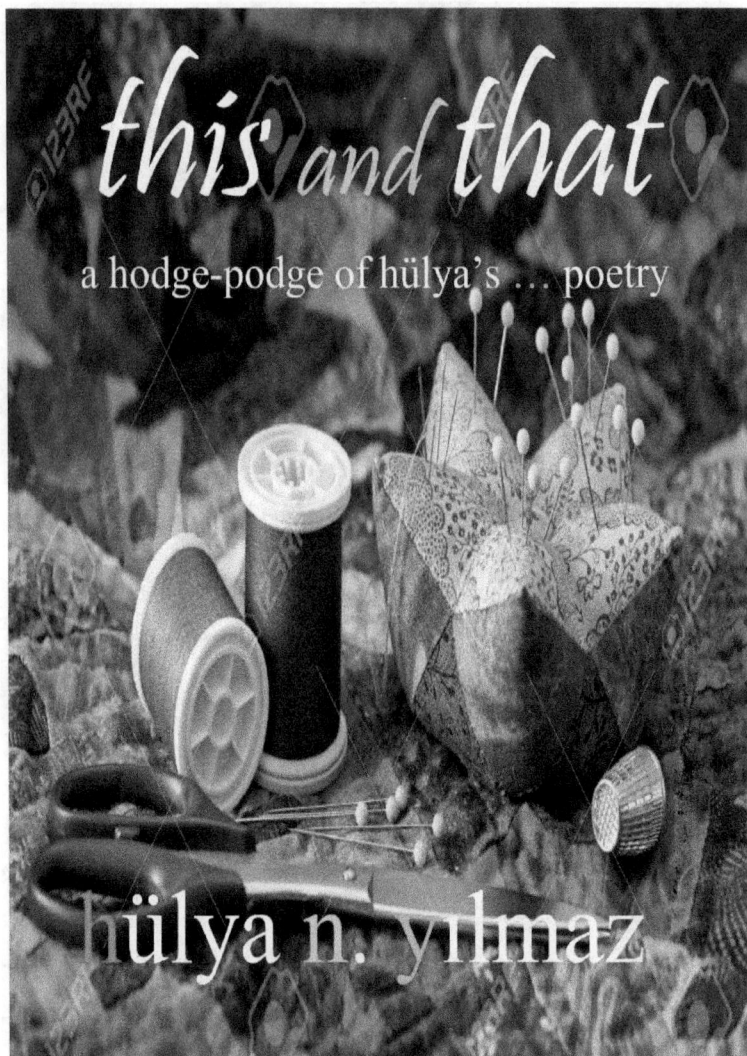

this and that

a hodge-podge of hülya's ... poetry

hülya n. yılmaz

Now Available at
www.innerchildpress.com

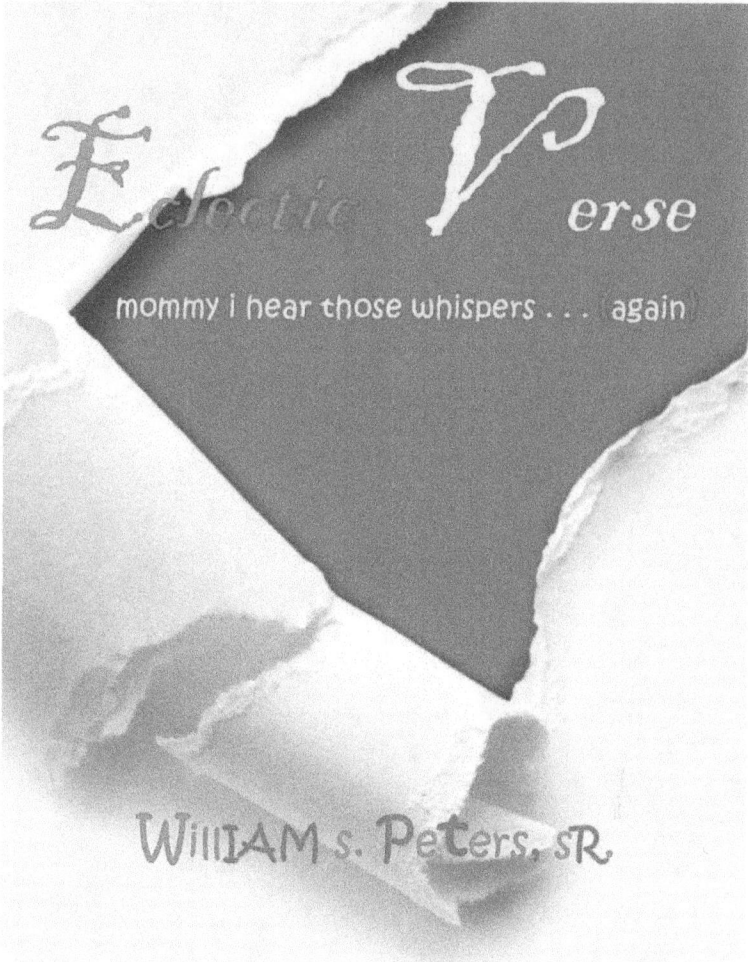

Eclectic Verse

mommy i hear those whispers . . . again

WilliAM s. Peters, sR

HERENOW

◆

FAHREDIN SHEHU

146

Now Available at
www.innerchildpress.com

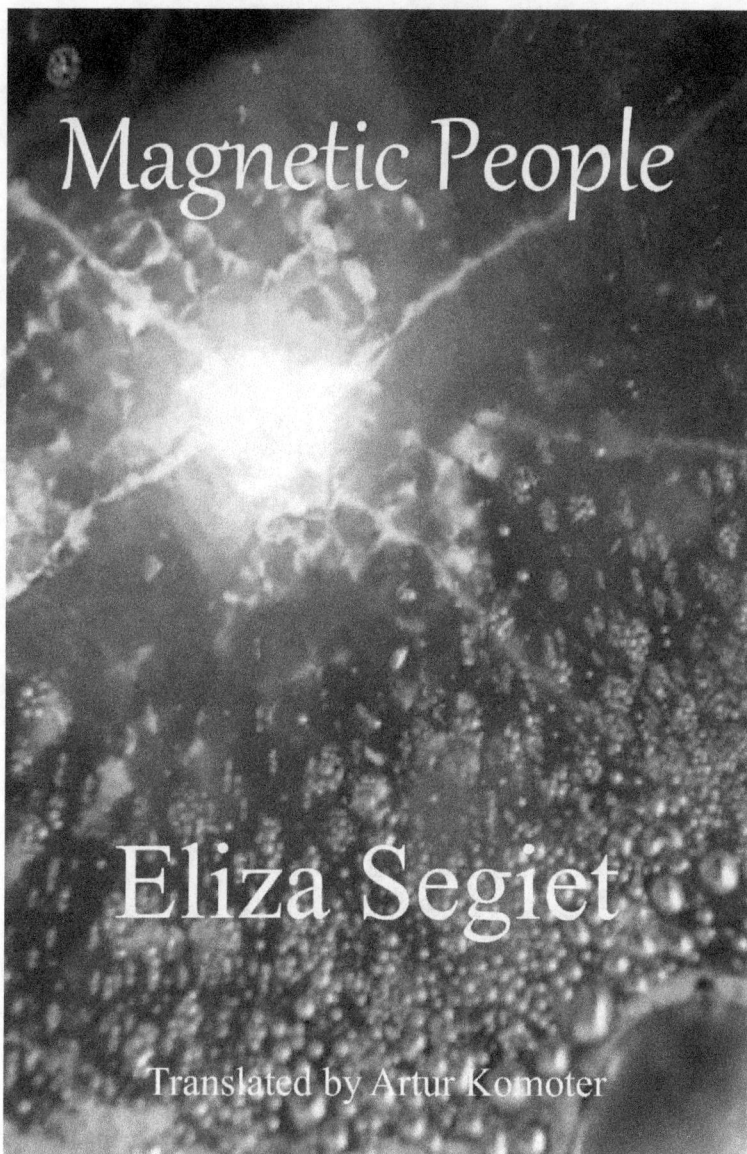

Magnetic People

Eliza Segiet

Translated by Artur Komoter

Now Available at
www.innerchildpress.com

Now Available at
www.innerchildpress.com

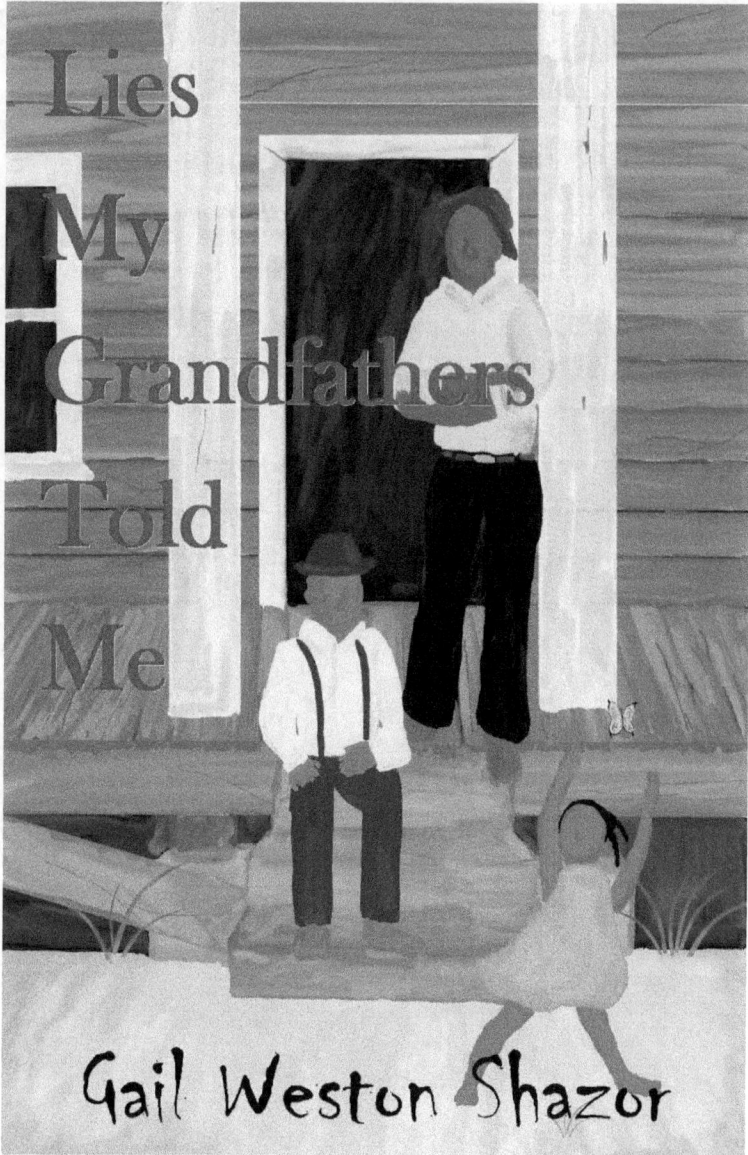

Lies
My
Grandfathers
Told
Me

Gail Weston Shazor

Now Available at
www.innerchildpress.com

Aflame

Memoirs in Verse

hülya n. yılmaz

Now Available at
www.innerchildpress.com

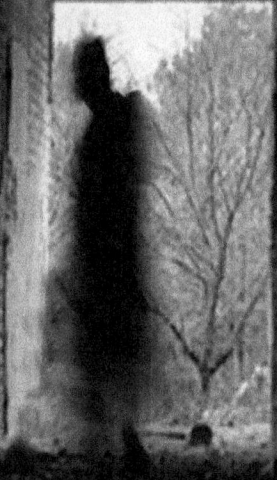

My Shadow

Nizar Sartawi

Now Available at
www.innerchildpress.com

Mass Graves

Faleeha Hassan

Now Available at
www.innerchildpress.com

Breakfast

for

Butterflies

Faleeha Hassan

Now Available at
www.innerchildpress.com

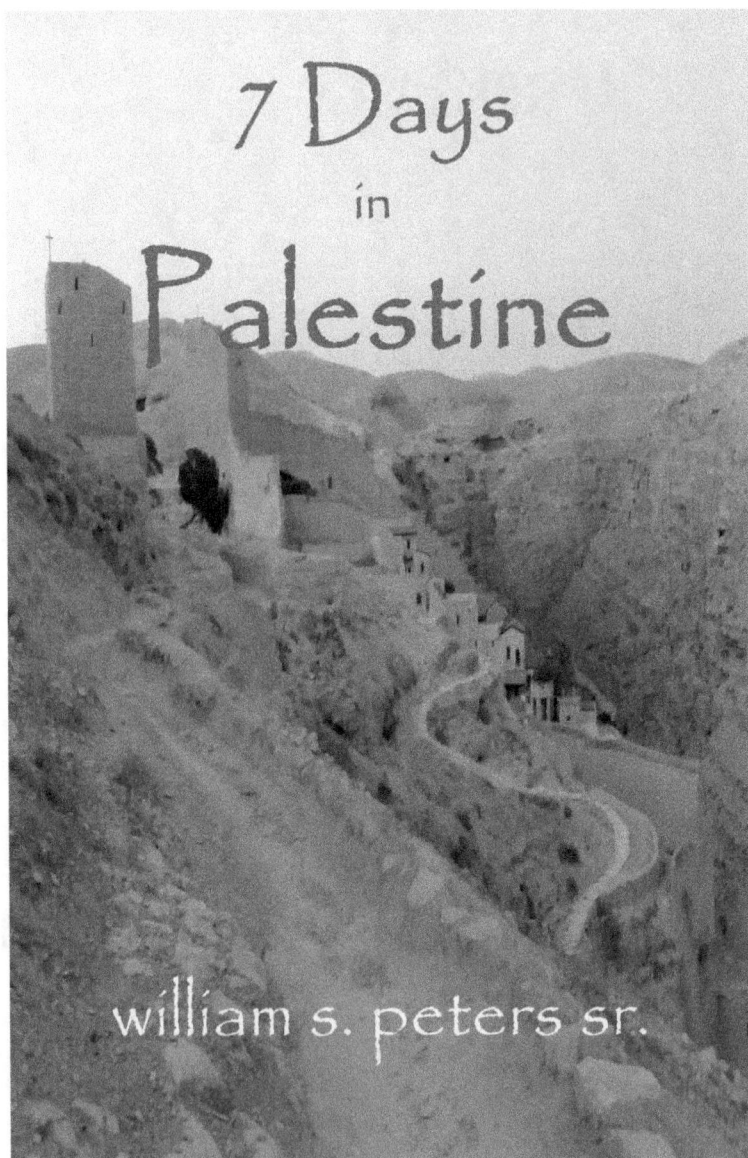

7 Days
in
Palestine

william s. peters sr.

Now Available at
www.innerchildpress.com

inner child press
presents

Tunisia My Love

william s. peters, sr.

Coming in the Summer of 2019

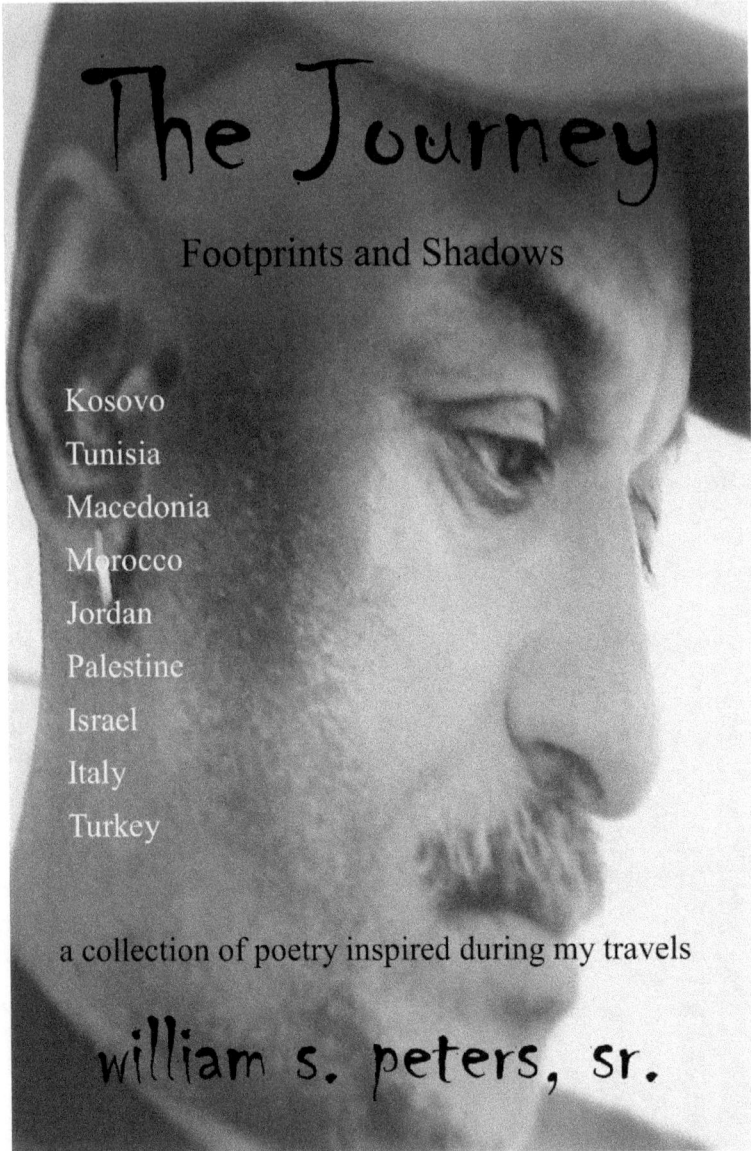

The Journey

Footprints and Shadows

Kosovo
Tunisia
Macedonia
Morocco
Jordan
Palestine
Israel
Italy
Turkey

a collection of poetry inspired during my travels

william s. peters, sr.

Now Available at
www.innerchildpress.com

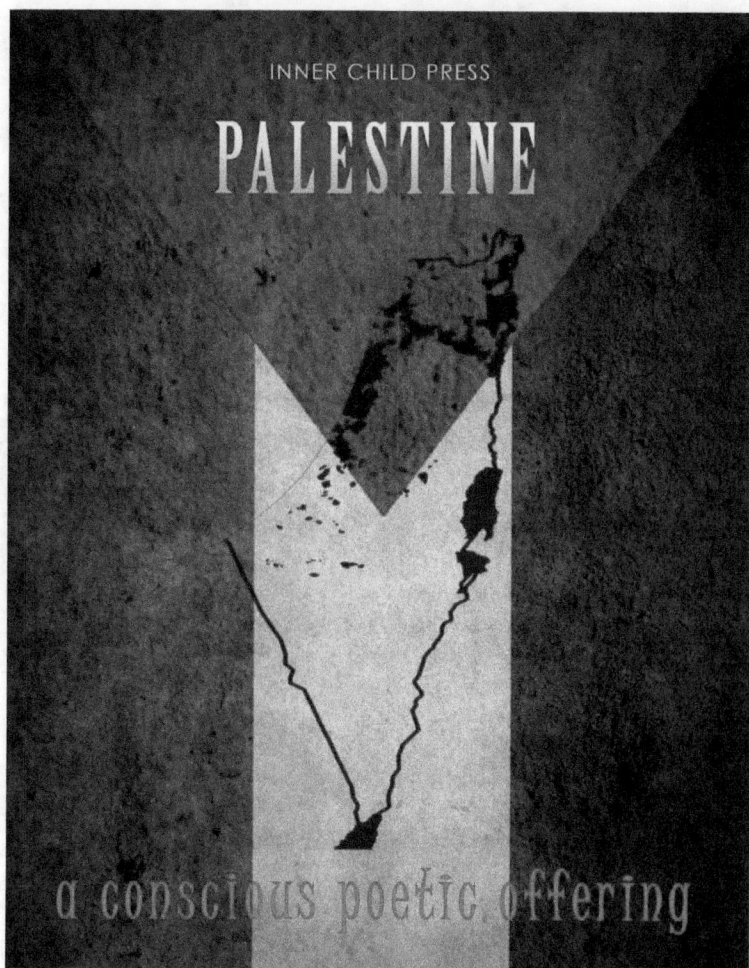

INNER CHILD PRESS

PALESTINE

a conscious poetic offering

Now Available at
www.innerchildpress.com

Now Available at

www.innerchildpress.com

INNER CHILD PRESS

THIS IS WHY I
SLEEP

william s. peters sr.

Now Available at

www.innerchildpress.com

Think on These Things
Book II

william s. peters, sr.

Now Available at
www.innerchildpress.com

Poetry
from the
Balkans

The Balkan Poets

Other

Anthological

works from

Inner Child Press International

www.innerchildpress.com

Inner Child Press International
presents

A Love Anthology
2019

The Love Poets

Now Available

www.worldhealingworldpeacepoetry.com

Now Available

www.worldhealingworldpeacepoetry.com

Now Available

www.worldhealingworldpeacepoetry.com

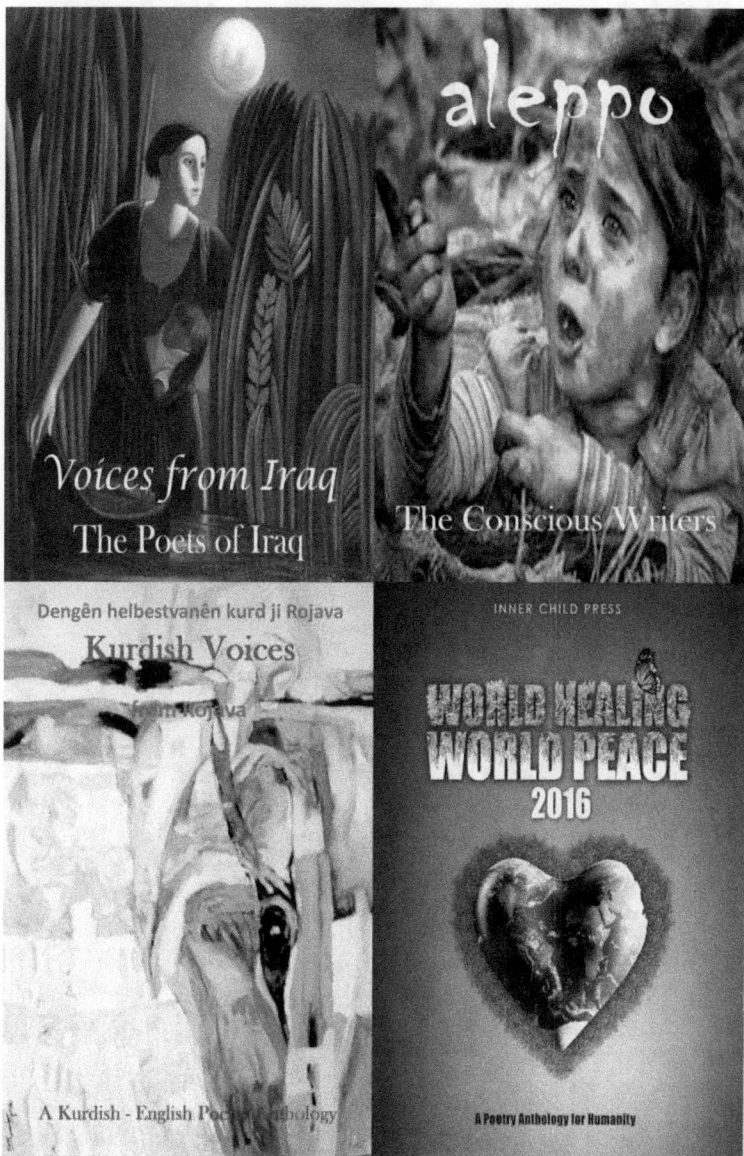

Now Available

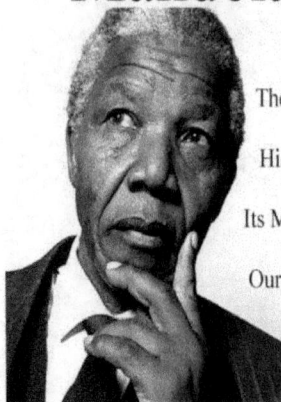

Mandela
The Man
His Life
Its Meaning
Our Words

Poetry . . . Commentary & Stories
The Anthological Writers

A GATHERING OF WORDS

POETRY & COMMENTARY
FOR
TRAYVON MARTIN

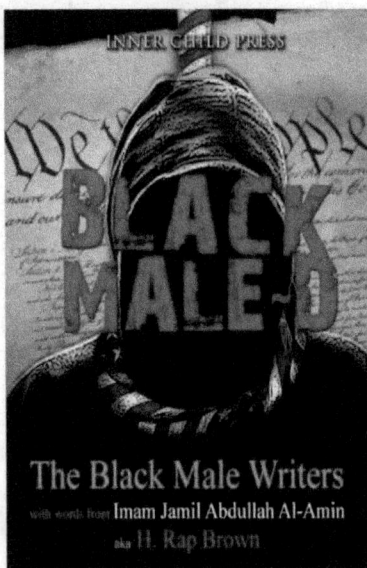

INNER CHILD PRESS

BLACK MALE-D

The Black Male Writers
with words from Imam Jamil Abdullah Al-Amin
aka H. Rap Brown

I
want
my
poetry
to... volume 4

the conscious poets
inspired by . . . Monte Smith

Now Available

www.innerchildpress.com/anthologies

Now Available

Now Available

Now Available

www.innerchildpress.com/anthologies

The Year of the Poet
January 2014

The Poetry Posse

Jamie Bond
Gail Weston Shazor
Albert 'Infinite' Carrasco
Siddartha Beth Pierce
Janet P. Caldwell
June 'Bugg' Barefield
Debbie M. Allen
Tony Henninger
Joe DaVerbal Minddancer
Robert Gibbons
Neetu Wali
Shareef Abdur-Rasheed
William S. Peters, Sr.

Carnation

Our January Feature
Terri L. Johnson

the Year of the Poet
February 2014

violets

The Poetry Posse

Jamie Bond
Gail Weston Shazor
Albert 'Infinite' Carrasco
Siddartha Beth Pierce
Janet P. Caldwell
June 'Bugg' Barefield
Debbie M. Allen
Tony Henninger
Joe DaVerbal Minddancer
Robert Gibbons
Neetu Wali
Shareef Abdur-Rasheed
William S. Peters, Sr.

Our February Features
Teresa E. Gallion & Robert Gibson

the Year of the Poet
March 2014

The Poetry Posse

Jamie Bond
Gail Weston Shazor
Albert 'Infinite' Carrasco
Siddartha Beth Pierce
Janet P. Caldwell
June 'Bugg' Barefield
Debbie M. Allen
Tony Henninger
Joe DaVerbal Minddancer
Robert Gibbons
Neetu Wali
Shareef Abdur-Rasheed
Kimberly Burnham
William S. Peters, Sr.

daffodil

Our March Featured Poets
AliciaC. Cooper & hülya yilmaz

the Year of the Poet
April 2014

The Poetry Posse

Jamie Bond
Gail Weston Shazor
Albert 'Infinite' Carrasco
Siddartha Beth Pierce
Janet P. Caldwell
June 'Bugg' Barefield
Debbie M. Allen
Tony Henninger
Joe DaVerbal Minddancer
Robert Gibbons
Neetu Wali
Shareef Abdur-Rasheed
William S. Peters, Sr.

Our April Featured Poets
Fahredin Shehu
Martina Reisz Newberry
Justin Blackburn
Monte Smith

celebrating international poetry month

Sweet Pea

Now Available

www.innerchildpress.com/the-year-of-the-poet

the year of the poet
May 2014

May's Featured Poets
ReeCee
Joski the Poet
Shannon Stanton

Dedicated to our Children

The Poetry Posse
Jamie Bond
Gail Weston Shazor
Albert Infinite Carrasco
Siddartha Beth Pierce
Janet P. Caldwell
Jamie 'Bugg' Barefield
Debbie M. Allen
Tony Henninger
Joe DeVerbal Minddancer
Robert Gibbons
Neetu Wali
Shareef Abdur-Rasheed
Kimberly Burnham
William S. Peters, Sr.

Lily of the Valley

the Year of the Poet
June 2014

Love & Relationship

Rose

June's Featured Poets
Shantelle McLin
Jacqueline D. R. Kennedy
Abraham N. Benjamin

The Poetry Posse
Jamie Bond
Gail Weston Shazor
Albert Infinite Carrasco
Siddartha Beth Pierce
Janet P. Caldwell
Jamie 'Bugg' Barefield
Debbie M. Allen
Tony Henninger
Joe DeVerbal Minddancer
Robert Gibbons
Neetu Wali
Shareef Abdur-Rasheed
Kimberly Burnham
William S. Peters, Sr.

The Year of the Poet
July 2014

July Feature Poets
Christena A. V. Williams
Dr. John R. Strum
Kolade Olanrewaju Freedom

The Poetry Posse
Jamie Bond
Gail Weston Shazor
Albert Infinite Carrasco
Siddartha Beth Pierce
Janet P. Caldwell
Jamie 'Bugg' Barefield
Debbie M. Allen
Tony Henninger
Joe DeVerbal Minddancer
Robert Gibbons
Neetu Wali
Shareef Abdur-Rasheed
Kimberly Burnham
William S. Peters, Sr.

Lotus
Asian Flower of the Month

The Year of the Poet
August 2014

Gladiolus

The Poetry Posse
Jamie Bond
Gail Weston Shazor
Albert Infinite Carrasco
Siddartha Beth Pierce
Janet P. Caldwell
Jamie 'Bugg' Barefield
Debbie M. Allen
Tony Henninger
Joe DeVerbal Minddancer
Robert Gibbons
Neetu Wali
Shareef Abdur-Rasheed
Kimberly Burnham
William S. Peters, Sr.

August Feature Poets
Ann White * Rosalind Cherry * Sheila Jenkins

Now Available

www.innerchildpress.com/the-year-of-the-poet

The Year of the Poet
September 2014

Aster   Morning-Glory

Wild Cyclamen September Birth Flower

September Feature Poets
Florence Malone * Keith Alan Hamilton

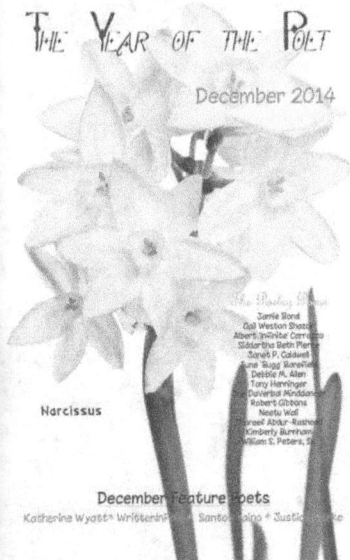

The Poetry Posse
Jamie Bond * Gail Weston Shazor * Albert 'Infinite' Carrasco * Siddartha Beth Pierce
Janet P. Caldwell * June 'Bugg' Barefield * Debbie M. Allen * Tony Henninger
Joe Dolverbul Minddancer * Robert Gibbons * Neetu Wali * Shareef Abdur-Rasheed
Kimberly Burnham * William S. Peters, Sr.

THE YEAR OF THE POET
October 2014

Red Poppy

The Poetry Posse
Jamie Bond * Gail Weston Shazor * Albert 'Infinite' Carrasco * Siddartha Beth Pierce
Janet P. Caldwell * June 'Bugg' Barefield * Debbie M. Allen * Tony Henninger
Joe Dolverbul Minddancer * Robert Gibbons * Neetu Wali * Shareef Abdur-Rasheed
Kimberly Burnham * William S. Peters, Sr.

October Feature Poets
Ceri Naz * Rajendra Padhi * Elizabeth Castillo

THE YEAR OF THE POET
November 2014

Chrysanthemum

The Poetry Posse
Jamie Bond * Gail Weston Shazor * Albert 'Infinite' Carrasco * Siddartha Beth Pierce
Janet P. Caldwell * June 'Bugg' Barefield * Debbie M. Allen * Tony Henninger
Joe Dolverbul Minddancer * Robert Gibbons * Neetu Wali * Shareef Abdur-Rasheed
Kimberly Burnham * William S. Peters, Sr.

November Feature Poets
Jocelyn Mosman * Jackie Allen * James Moore * Neville Hiatt

THE YEAR OF THE POET
December 2014

Narcissus

The Poetry Posse
Jamie Bond
Gail Weston Shazor
Albert 'Infinite' Carrasco
Siddartha Beth Pierce
Janet P. Caldwell
June 'Bugg' Barefield
Debbie M. Allen
Tony Henninger
Dolverbul Minddancer
Robert Gibbons
Neetu Wali
Shareef Abdur-Rasheed
Kimberly Burnham
William S. Peters, Sr.

December Feature Poets
Katherine Wyatt* Wristenbri Santos Lopo * Justi   e

Now Available

www.innerchildpress.com/the-year-of-the-poet

THE YEAR OF THE POET II
January 2015

The Poetry Posse

Garnet

Jamie Bond
Gail Weston Shazor
Albert 'Infinite' Carrasco
Siddartha Beth Pierce
Janet P. Caldwell
Tony Henninger
Joe DaVerbal Minddancer
Robert Gibbons
Neetu Wali
Shareef Abdur ~ Rasheed
Kimberly Burnham
Ann White
Keith Alan Hamilton
Katherine Wyatt
Fahredin Shehu
Hülya N. Yılmaz
Teresa E. Gallion
Jackie Allen
William S. Peters, Sr.

January Feature Poets
Bismay Mohanti * Jen Walls * Eric Judah

THE YEAR OF THE POET II
February 2015

Amethyst

THE POETRY POSSE

Jamie Bond
Gail Weston Shazor
Albert 'Infinite' Carrasco
Siddartha Beth Pierce
Janet P. Caldwell
Tony Henninger
Joe DaVerbal Minddancer
Robert Gibbons
Neetu Wali
Shareef Abdur ~ Rasheed
Kimberly Burnham
Ann White
Keith Alan Hamilton
Katherine Wyatt
Fahredin Shehu
Hülya N. Yılmaz
Teresa E. Gallion
Jackie Allen
William S. Peters, Sr.

FEBRUARY FEATURE POETS
Iram Fatima * Bob McNeil * Kerstin Centervall

The Year of the Poet II
March 2015

Our Featured Poets

Heung Sook * Anthony Arnold * Alicia Foland

Bloodstone

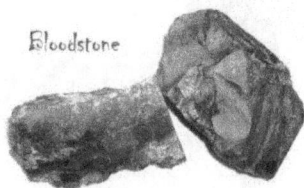

The Poetry Posse 2015
Jamie Bond * Gail Weston Shazor * Albert 'Infinite' Carrasco
Siddartha Beth Pierce * Janet P. Caldwell * Tony Henninger
Joe DaVerbal Minddancer * Neetu Wali * Shareef Abdur ~ Rasheed
Kimberly Burnham * Ann White * Keith Alan Hamilton
Katherine Wyatt * Fahredin Shehu * Hülya N. Yılmaz
Teresa E. Gallion * Jackie Allen * William S. Peters, Sr

The Year of the Poet II
April 2015

Celebrating International Poetry Month

Our Featured Poets

Raja Williams * Dennis Ferado * Laure Charazac

Diamonds

The Poetry Posse 2015
Jamie Bond * Gail Weston Shazor * Albert 'Infinite' Carrasco
Siddartha Beth Pierce * Janet P. Caldwell * Tony Henninger
Joe DaVerbal Minddancer * Neetu Wali * Shareef Abdur ~ Rasheed
Kimberly Burnham * Ann White * Keith Alan Hamilton
Katherine Wyatt * Fahredin Shehu * Hülya N. Yılmaz
Teresa E. Gallion * Jackie Allen * William S. Peters, Sr

Now Available

www.innerchildpress.com/the-year-of-the-poet

The Year of the Poet II
May 2015

May's Featured Poets

Geri Algeri
Akin Moú Chinnery
Anna Jakubeza

Emeralds

The Poetry Posse 2015

Jamie Bond * Gail Weston Shazor * Albert 'Infinite' Carrasco
Siddartha Beth Pierce * Janet P. Caldwell * Tony Henninger
Joe DaVerbal Minddancer * Neetu Wali * Shareef Abdur – Rasheed
Kimberly Burnham * Ann White * Keith Alan Hamilton
Katherine Wyatt * Fahredin Shehu * Hülya N. Yılmaz
Teresa E. Gallion * Jackie Allen * William S. Peters, Sr.

The Year of the Poet II
June 2015

June's Featured Poets

Anahit Arustamyan * Yvette D. Murrell * Ragina A. Walker

Pearl

The Poetry Posse 2015

Jamie Bond * Gail Weston Shazor * Albert 'Infinite' Carrasco
Siddartha Beth Pierce * Janet P. Caldwell * Tony Henninger
Joe DaVerbal Minddancer * Neetu Wali * Shareef Abdur – Rasheed
Kimberly Burnham * Ann White * Keith Alan Hamilton
Katherine Wyatt * Fahredin Shehu * Hülya N. Yılmaz
Teresa E. Gallion * Jackie Allen * William S. Peters, Sr.

The Year of the Poet II
July 2015

The Featured Poets for July 2015

Abhik Shome * Christina Neal * Robert Neal

Rubies

The Poetry Posse 2015

Jamie Bond * Gail Weston Shazor * Albert 'Infinite' Carrasco
Siddartha Beth Pierce * Janet P. Caldwell * Tony Henninger
Joe DaVerbal Minddancer * Neetu Wali * Shareef Abdur – Rasheed
Kimberly Burnham * Ann White * Keith Alan Hamilton
Katherine Wyatt * Fahredin Shehu * Hülya N. Yılmaz
Teresa E. Gallion * Jackie Allen * William S. Peters, Sr.

The Year of the Poet II
August 2015

Peridot

Featured Poets

Gayle Howell
Ann Chalasz
Christopher Schultz

The Poetry Posse 2015

Jamie Bond * Gail Weston Shazor * Albert 'Infinite' Carrasco
Siddartha Beth Pierce * Janet P. Caldwell * Tony Henninger
Joe DaVerbal Minddancer * Neetu Wali * Shareef Abdur – Rasheed
Kimberly Burnham * Ann White * Keith Alan Hamilton
Katherine Wyatt * Fahredin Shehu * Hülya N. Yılmaz
Teresa E. Gallion * Jackie Allen * William S. Peters, Sr.

Now Available

www.innerchildpress.com/the-year-of-the-poet

176

The Year of the Poet III
January 2016
Featured Poets
Lana Joseph * Atom Cyrus Rush * Christena Williams
Dark-eyed Junco
The Poetry Posse 2016

The Year of the Poet III
February 2016
Featured Poets
Anthony Arnold
Anna Chalasz
Andre Hawthorne
Puffin
The Poetry Posse 2016

The Year of the Poet
March 2016
Featured Poets
Jeton Kelmendi   Nizar Sartawi   Sami Muhanna
Robin
The Poetry Posse 2016

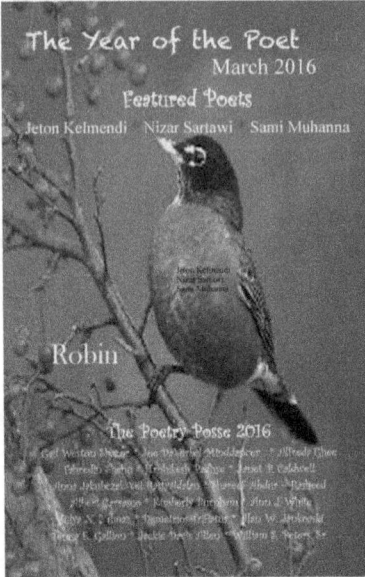

The Year of the Poet III
Featured Poets
Ali Abdolrezaei
Anna Chalasz
Agim Vinca
Ceri Naz
Black Capped Chickadee
The Poetry Posse 2016
celebrating international poetry month

Now Available

www.innerchildpress.com/the-year-of-the-poet

The Year of the Poet
May 2016

Bob Strum
Barbara Allan
D.L. Davis

Oriole

Gail Weston Shazor * Joe DaVerbal Minddancer * Alfreda Ghee
Nizar Sartawi * Hülya Yılmaz * Janet P. Caldwell
Anna Jakubczak Vel RattyAdalan * Shareef Abdur - Rasheed
Albert Carrasco * Kimberly Burnham * Ken J. White
Hülya N. Yılmaz * Demetrios Trifiatis * Alan W. Jankowski
Teresa E. Gallion * Jackie Davis Allen * William S. Peters, Sr.

The Year of the Poet III
June 2016

Featured Poets

Qibrije Demiri- Frangu
Naime Beqiraj
Faleeha Hassan
Bedri Zyberaj

Black Necked Stilt

The Poetry Posse 2016

Gail Weston Shazor * Joe DaVerbal Minddancer * Alfreda Ghee
Nizar Sartawi * Hülya Yılmaz * Janet P. Caldwell
Anna Jakubczak Vel RattyAdalan * Shareef Abdur - Rasheed
Albert Carrasco * Kimberly Burnham * Ken J. White
Hülya N. Yılmaz * Demetrios Trifiatis * Alan W. Jankowski
Teresa E. Gallion * Jackie Davis Allen * William S. Peters, Sr.

The Year of the Poet III
July 2016

Tram Fatima 'Ashi
Langley Shazor
Jody Doty
Emilia T. Davis

Indigo Bunting

The Poetry Posse 2016

The Year of the Poet III
August 2016

Featured Poets

Anita Dash
Irena Jovanovic
Malgorzata Gouluda

Painted Bunting

The Poetry Posse 2016

Now Available

www.innerchildpress.com/the-year-of-the-poet

The Year of the Poet III
September 2016

Featured Poets
Simone Weber
Abhijit Sen
Eunice Barbara C. Novio

Long Billed Curlew

The Poetry Posse 2016

The Year of the Poet III
October 2016

Featured Poets
Lina Joseph
Krishnamurthy R
James Moore

Barn Owl

The Poetry Posse 2016

The Year of the Poet III
November 2016

Featured Poets
Rosemary Burns
Robin Ouzman Hislop
Lonneice Weeks-Badley

Northern Cardinal

The Poetry Posse 2016

The Year of the Poet III
December 2016

Featured Poets
Samih Masoud
Mountassir Aziz Bien
Abdulkadir Musa

Rough Legged Hawk

The Poetry Posse 2016

Now Available

www.innerchildpress.com/the-year-of-the-poet

The Year of the Poet IV
January 2017

Featured Poets

Jon Winell
Natalie Shields
Irani Fatima Ashi

Quaking Aspen

The Poetry Posse 2017

Gail Weston Shazor * Caroline Nazareno * Jhumy Mohanty
Nizar Sartawi * Anna Jakubczak Vel Ratty Adalan * Jen Walls
Joe DaVerbal Minddancer * Shareef Abdur – Rasheed
Albert Carrasco * Kimberly Burnham * Elizabeth Castillo
Hülya N. Yılmaz * Teresa Hassen * Alan W. Jankowski
Teresa E. Gallion * Jackie Davis Allen * William S. Peters, Sr.

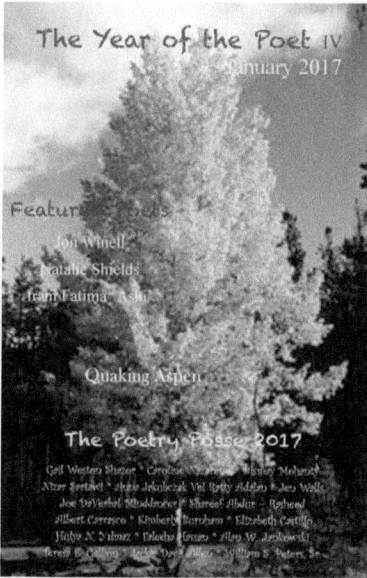

The Year of the Poet IV
February 2017

Featured Poets

Lin Ross
Souleima Falhi
Anwer Ghani

Witch Hazel

The Poetry Posse 2017

Gail Weston Shazor * Caroline Nazareno * Jhumy Mohanty
Nizar Sartawi * Anna Jakubczak Vel Ratty Adalan * Jen Walls
Joe DaVerbal Minddancer * Shareef Abdur – Rasheed
Albert Carrasco * Kimberly Burnham * Elizabeth Castillo
Hülya N. Yılmaz * Teresa Hassen * Alan W. Jankowski
Teresa E. Gallion * Jackie Davis Allen * William S. Peters, Sr.

The Year of the Poet IV
March 2017

Featured Poets

Tremell Stevens
Francisca Richinski
Jamil Abu Shaih

The Eastern Redbud

The Poetry Posse 2017

Gail Weston Shazor * Caroline Nazareno * Jhumy Mohanty
Teresa E. Gallion * Anna Jakubczak Vel Ratty Adalan
Joe DaVerbal Minddancer * Shareef Abdur – Rasheed
Albert Carrasco * Kimberly Burnham * Elizabeth Castillo
Hülya N. Yılmaz * Teresa Hassen * Jackie Davis Allen
Jen Walls * Nizar Sartawi * * William S. Peters, Sr.

The Year of the Poet IV
April 2017

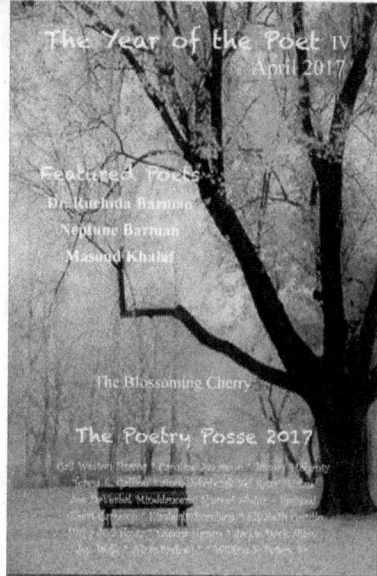

Featured Poets

Dr. Ruchida Barman
Neptune Barman
Masood Khalaf

The Blossoming Cherry

The Poetry Posse 2017

Gail Weston Shazor * Caroline Nazareno * Jhumy Mohanty
Teresa E. Gallion * Anna Jakubczak Vel Ratty Adalan
Joe DaVerbal Minddancer * Shareef Abdur – Rasheed
Albert Carrasco * Kimberly Burnham * Elizabeth Castillo
Hülya N. Yılmaz * Teresa Hassen * Jackie Davis Allen
Jen Walls * Nizar Sartawi * * William S. Peters, Sr.

Now Available

www.innerchildpress.com/the-year-of-the-poet

The Year of the Poet IV
May 2017

The Flowering Dogwood Tree

Featured Poets
Kallisa Powell
Alicja Maria Kuberska
Fethi Sassi

The Poetry Posse 2017

Gail Weston Shazor * Caroline Nazareno * Teresa E. Gallion * Anne Jakubczak, Val Ketty Adekto Joe DaVerbal Minddancer * Shareef Abdur – Rasheed Albert Carrasco * Kimberly Burnham * Elizabeth Castillo Hülya N. Yılmaz * Faleeha Hassan * Jackie Davis Allen Jen Walls * Nizar Sartawi * * William S. Peters, Sr.

The Year of the Poet IV
June 2017

Featured Poets
Eliza Segiet
Tze-Min Tsai
Abdulla Issa

The Linden Tree

The Poetry Posse 2017

The Year of the Poet IV
July 2017

Featured Poets
Anca Mihaela Bruma
Ibaa Ismail
Zvonko Taneski

The Oak Moon

The Poetry Posse 2017

The Year of the Poet IV
August 2017

Featured Poets
Jonathan Aquino
Kitty Hsu
Langley Shazor

The Hazelnut Tree

The Poetry Posse 2017

Gail Weston Shazor * Caroline Nazareno * Teresa E. Gallion * Anne Jakubczak, Val Ketty Adekto Joe DaVerbal Minddancer * Shareef Abdur – Rasheed Albert Carrasco * Kimberly Burnham * Elizabeth Castillo Hülya N. Yılmaz * Faleeha Hassan * Jackie Davis Allen Jen Walls * Nizar Sartawi * * William S. Peters, Sr.

Now Available

www.innerchildpress.com/the-year-of-the-poet

The Year of the Poet IV
September 2017

Featured Poets

Martina Reisz Newberry
Ameer Nassir
Christine Fulco Neal
Robert Neal

The Elm Tree

The Poetry Posse 2017

Gail Weston Shazor * Caroline Nazareno * Bismay Mohanty
Teresa E. Gallion * Anna Jakubczak Vel Ratty Adalan
Joe DaVerbal Minddancer * Shareef Abdur – Rasheed
Albert Carrasco * Kimberly Burnham * Elizabeth Castillo
Hülya N. Yılmaz * Faleeha Hassan * Jackie Davis Allen
Jen Walls * Nizar Sartawi * * William S. Peters, Sr.

The Year of the Poet IV
October 2017

Featured Poets

Ahmed Abu Saleem
Nedal Al-Qaeim
Sadeddin Shahin

The Black Walnut Tree

The Poetry Posse 2017

Gail Weston Shazor * Caroline Nazareno * Bismay Mohanty
Teresa E. Gallion * Anna Jakubczak Vel Ratty Adalan
Joe DaVerbal Minddancer * Shareef Abdur – Rasheed
Albert Carrasco * Kimberly Burnham * Elizabeth Castillo
Hülya N. Yılmaz * Faleeha Hassan * Jackie Davis Allen
Jen Walls * Nizar Sartawi * * William S. Peters, Sr.

The Year of the Poet IV
November 2017

Featured Poets

Kay Peters
Alfreda D. Ghee
Gabriella Garofalo
Rosemary Cappello

The Tree of Life

The Poetry Posse 2017

Gail Weston Shazor * Caroline Nazareno * Bismay Mohanty
Teresa E. Gallion * Anna Jakubczak Vel Ratty Adalan
Joe DaVerbal Minddancer * Shareef Abdur – Rasheed
Albert Carrasco * Kimberly Burnham * Elizabeth Castillo
Hülya N. Yılmaz * Faleeha Hassan * Jackie Davis Allen
Jen Walls * Nizar Sartawi * William S. Peters, Sr.

The Year of the Poet IV
December 2017

Featured Poets

Justice Clarke
Mariel M. Pabroa
Kiley Brown

The Fig Tree

The Poetry Posse 2017

Gail Weston Shazor * Caroline Nazareno * Bismay Mohanty
Teresa E. Gallion * Anna Jakubczak Vel Ratty Adalan
Joe DaVerbal Minddancer * Shareef Abdur – Rasheed
Albert Carrasco * Kimberly Burnham * Elizabeth Castillo
Hülya N. Yılmaz * Faleeha Hassan * Jackie Davis Allen
Jen Walls * Nizar Sartawi * William S. Peters, Sr.

Now Available

www.innerchildpress.com/the-year-of-the-poet

The Year of the Poet V
January 2018
Featured Poets
Iyad Shamasnah
Yasmeen Hamzeh
Ali Abdolrezaei

Aksum

The Poetry Posse 2018
Gail Weston Shazor * Caroline Nazareno * Tezmin Ition Tsai
Hülya N. Yılmaz * Faleeha Hassan * Jackie Davis Allen
Teresa E. Gallion * Anna Jakubczak Vel Ratty Adalan
Alicja Maria Kuberska * Shareef Abdur – Rasheed
Kimberly Burnham * Elizabeth Castillo
Nizar Sartawi * William S. Peters, Sr.

The Year of the Poet V
February 2018

Sabean

Featured Poets
Muhammad Azram
Anna Szawrncka
Abhilipsa Kuanar
Aanika Aery

The Poetry Posse 2018
Gail Weston Shazor * Caroline Nazareno * Tezmin Ition Tsai
Hülya N. Yılmaz * Faleeha Hassan * Jackie Davis Allen
Teresa E. Gallion * Anna Jakubczak Vel Ratty Adalan
Alicja Maria Kuberska * Shareef Abdur – Rasheed
Kimberly Burnham * Elizabeth Castillo
Nizar Sartawi * William S. Peters, Sr.

The Year of the Poet V
March 2018

Featured Poets
Iram Fatima 'Ashi'
Cassandra Swan
Jaleel Khazaal
Sharia Zaman

Mexico
Cuba
Belize
Jamaica
Dominican Republic
Guatemala
Honduras
Haiti
Puerto Rico
El Salvador
Nicaragua
Costa Rica
Panama
Caribbean
&
Middle America

The Poetry Posse 2018
Gail Weston Shazor * Nizar Sartawi * Hülya N. Yılmaz
Jackie Davis Allen * Caroline 'Ceri' Nazareno
Alicja Maria Kuberska * Teresa E. Gallion
Faleeha Hassan * Shareef Abdur – Rasheed
Kimberly Burnham * Elizabeth Castillo
Tezmin Ition Tsai * William S. Peters, Sr.

The Year of the Poet V
April 2018

Featured Poets

The Nez Perce

The Poetry Posse 2018

Now Available

www.innerchildpress.com/the-year-of-the-poet

The Year of the Poet V
May 2018

Featured Poets

Zaidy Carreon de Leon &
Sylwia K. Malinowska
Emilia Ahmeti
Hebe Prodan

The Sumerians

The Poetry Posse 2018

Gail Weston Shazor * Nizar Sartawi * Hülya N. Yılmaz
Jackie Davis Allen * Caroline 'Ceri' Nazareno
Alicja Maria Kuberska * Teresa E. Gallion
Kimberly Burnham * Shareef Abdur – Rasheed
Faleeha Hassan * Elizabeth Castillo * Swapna Behera
Tezmin Ition Tsai * William S. Peters, Sr.

The Year of the Poet V
June 2018

Featured Poets

Bilall Maliqi * Daim Miftari * Gojko Božović * Sofija Živković

The Paleo Indians

The Poetry Posse 2018

Gail Weston Shazor * Nizar Sartawi * Hülya N. Yılmaz
Jackie Davis Allen * Caroline 'Ceri' Nazareno
Alicja Maria Kuberska * Teresa E. Gallion
Kimberly Burnham * Shareef Abdur – Rasheed
Faleeha Hassan * Elizabeth Castillo * Swapna Behera
Tezmin Ition Tsai * William S. Peters, Sr.

The Year of the Poet V
July 2018

Featured Poets
Padmaja Iyengar-Paddy
Mohammad Ikbal Hami
Eliza Segiet
Tom Higgins

Oceania

The Poetry Posse 2018

Gail Weston Shazor * Nizar Sartawi * Hülya N. Yılmaz
Jackie Davis Allen * Caroline 'Ceri' Nazareno
Alicja Maria Kuberska * Teresa E. Gallion
Kimberly Burnham * Shareef Abdur – Rasheed
Faleeha Hassan * Elizabeth Castillo * Swapna Behera
Tezmin Ition Tsai * William S. Peters, Sr.

The Year of the Poet V
August 2018

Featured Poets
Hussein Habasch * Mircea Dan Duta * Naida Mujkić * Swagat Das

The Lapita

The Poetry Posse 2018

Gail Weston Shazor * Nizar Sartawi * Hülya N. Yılmaz
Jackie Davis Allen * Caroline 'Ceri' Nazareno
Alicja Maria Kuberska * Teresa E. Gallion
Kimberly Burnham * Shareef Abdur – Rasheed
Ashok K. Bhargava* Elizabeth Castillo * Swapna Behera
Tezmin Ition Tsai * William S. Peters, Sr.

Now Available

www.innerchildpress.com/the-year-of-the-poet

The Year of the Poet V
September 2018

The Aztecs & Incas

Featured Poets
Kolade Olanrewaju Freedom
Eliza Segiet
Mazhar Hussan Abdul Ghani
Lily Swarn

The Poetry Posse 2018

Gail Weston Shazor * Nizar Sartawi * Hülya N. Yılmaz
Jackie Davis Allen * Caroline 'Ceri' Nazareno
Alicja Maria Kuberska * Teresa E. Gallion
Kimberly Burnham * Shareef Abdur – Rasheed
Ashok K. Bhargava * Elizabeth Castillo * Swapna Behera
Tezmin Ition Tsai * William S. Peters, Sr.

The Year of the Poet V
October 2018

Featured Poets
Alicia Minjarez * Lonneice Weeks-Badley
Lopamudra Mishra * Abdelwahed Souayah

Bengali

The Poetry Posse 2018

Gail Weston Shazor * Nizar Sartawi * Hülya N. Yılmaz
Jackie Davis Allen * Caroline 'Ceri' Nazareno
Alicja Maria Kuberska * Teresa E. Gallion
Kimberly Burnham * Shareef Abdur – Rasheed
Ashok K. Bhargava * Elizabeth Castillo * Swapna Behera
Tezmin Ition Tsai * William S. Peters, Sr.

The Year of the Poet V
November 2018

Featured Poets
Michelle Joan Barulich * Monsif Beroual
Krystyna Konecka * Nassira Nezzar

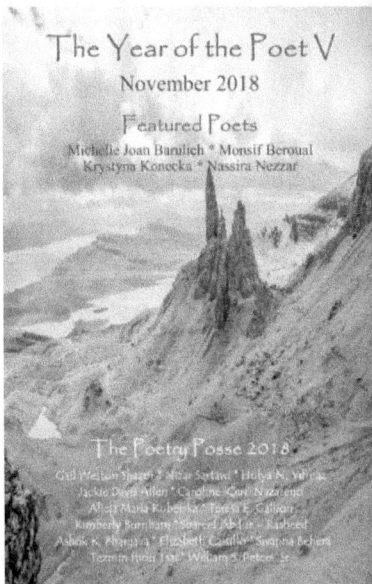

The Poetry Posse 2018

Gail Weston Shazor * Nizar Sartawi * Hülya N. Yılmaz
Jackie Davis Allen * Caroline 'Ceri' Nazareno
Alicja Maria Kuberska * Teresa E. Gallion
Kimberly Burnham * Shareef Abdur – Rasheed
Ashok K. Bhargava * Elizabeth Castillo * Swapna Behera
Tezmin Ition Tsai * William S. Peters, Sr.

The Year of the Poet V
December 2018

Featured Poets
Rose Terranova Cirigliano
Joanna Kalinowska
Sokolović Emir
Dr. T. Ashok Chakravarthy

The Maori

Gail Weston Shazor * Nizar Sartawi * Hülya N. Yılmaz
Jackie Davis Allen * Caroline 'Ceri' Nazareno
Alicja Maria Kuberska * Teresa E. Gallion
Kimberly Burnham * Shareef Abdur – Rasheed
Ashok K. Bhargava * Elizabeth Castillo * Swapna Behera
Tezmin Ition Tsai * William S. Peters, Sr.

Now Available

www.innerchildpress.com/the-year-of-the-poet

The Year of the Poet VI

January 2019

Indigenous North Americans

Featured Poets

Houda Elfchtali
Anthony Briscoe
Iram Fatima 'Ashi'
Dr. K. K. Mathew

Dream Catcher

The Poetry Posse 2019

Gail Weston Shazor * Joe Paire * Hülya N. Yılmaz
Jackie Davis Allen * Caroline 'Ceri' Nazareno
Alicja Maria Kuberska * Teresa E. Gallion
Kimberly Burnham * Shareef Abdur – Rasheed
Ashok K. Bhargava * Elizabeth Castillo * Swapna Behera
Tezmin Ition Tsai * William S. Peters, Sr.

The Year of the Poet VI

February 2019

Featured Poets

Marek Lukaszewicz * Bharati Nayak
Aida G. Roque * Jean-Jacques Fournier

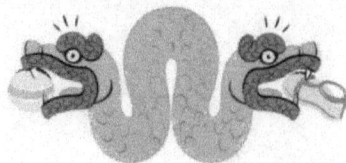

Meso-America

The Poetry Posse 2019

Gail Weston Shazor * Albert Carrasco * Hülya N. Yılmaz
Jackie Davis Allen * Caroline Nazareno * Eliza Segiet
Alicja Maria Kuberska * Teresa E. Gallion * Joe Paire
Kimberly Burnham * Shareef Abdur – Rasheed
Ashok K. Bhargava * Elizabeth Castillo * Swapna Behera
Tezmin Ition Tsai * William S. Peters, Sr.

The Year of the Poet VI

March 2019

Featured Poets

Enesa Mahmić * Sylwia K. Malinowska
Shurouk Hammoud * Anwer Ghani

The Caribbean

The Poetry Posse 2019

Gail Weston Shazor * Albert Carrasco * Hülya N. Yılmaz
Jackie Davis Allen * Caroline Nazareno * Eliza Segiet
Alicja Maria Kuberska * Teresa E. Gallion * Joe Paire
Kimberly Burnham * Shareef Abdur – Rasheed
Ashok K. Bhargava * Elizabeth Castillo * Swapna Behera
Tezmin Ition Tsai * William S. Peters, Sr.

The Year of the Poet VI

April 2019

Featured Poets

DL Davis * Michelle Joan Barulich
Lulëzim Haziri * Faleeha Hassan

Central & West Africa

The Poetry Posse 2019

Gail Weston Shazor * Albert Carrasco * Hülya N. Yılmaz
Jackie Davis Allen * Caroline Nazareno * Eliza Segiet
Alicja Maria Kuberska * Teresa E. Gallion * Joe Paire
Kimberly Burnham * Shareef Abdur – Rasheed
Ashok K. Bhargava * Elizabeth Castillo * Swapna Behera
Tezmin Ition Tsai * William S. Peters, Sr.

Now Available

www.innerchildpress.com/the-year-of-the-poet

The Year of the Poet VI
May 2019

Featured Poets

Emad Al-Haydary * Hussein Nasser Jabr
Wahab Sheriff * Abdul Razzaq Al Ameeri

Asia Southeast Asia and Maritime Asia

The Poetry Posse 2019

Gail Weston Shazor * Albert Carrasco * Hülya N. Yılmaz
Jackie Davis Allen * Caroline Nazareno * Eliza Segiet
Alicja Maria Kuberska * Teresa E. Gallion * Joe Paire
Kimberly Burnham * Shareef Abdur – Rasheed
Ashok K. Bhargava * Elizabeth Castillo * Swapna Behera
Tezmin Ition Tsai * William S. Peters, Sr.

The Year of the Poet VI
June 2019

Featured Poets

Kate Gandi Powiekszone * Sahaj Sabharwal
Iwu Jeff * Mohamed Abdel Aziz Shmeis

Arctic
Circumpolar

The Poetry Posse 2019

Gail Weston Shazor * Albert Carrasco * Hülya N. Yılmaz
Jackie Davis Allen * Caroline Nazareno * Eliza Segiet
Alicja Maria Kuberska * Teresa E. Gallion * Joe Paire
Kimberly Burnham * Shareef Abdur – Rasheed
Ashok K. Bhargava * Elizabeth Castillo * Swapna Behera
Tezmin Ition Tsai * William S. Peters, Sr.

The Year of the Poet VI

Featured Poets

Saadeddin Shahin * Andy Scott
Fahredin Shehu * Alok Kumar Ray

The Horn of Africa

Ethiopia   Djibouti

Somalia   Eritrea

The Poetry Posse 2019

Gail Weston Shazor * Albert Carrasco * Hülya N. Yılmaz
Jackie Davis Allen * Caroline Nazareno * Eliza Segiet
Alicja Maria Kuberska * Teresa E. Gallion * Joe Paire
Kimberly Burnham * Shareef Abdur – Rasheed
Ashok K. Bhargava * Elizabeth Castillo * Swapna Behera
Tezmin Ition Tsai * William S. Peters, Sr.

The Year of the Poet VI
August 2019

Featured Poets

Shola Balogun * Bharati Nayak
Monalisa Dash Dwibedy * Mbizo Chirasha

Coexist

Southwest Asia

The Poetry Posse 2019

Gail Weston Shazor * Albert Carrasco * Hülya N. Yılmaz
Jackie Davis Allen * Caroline Nazareno * Eliza Segiet
Alicja Maria Kuberska * Teresa E. Gallion * Joe Paire
Kimberly Burnham * Shareef Abdur – Rasheed
Ashok K. Bhargava * Elizabeth Castillo * Swapna Behera
Tezmin Ition Tsai * William S. Peters, Sr.

Now Available

www.innerchildpress.com/the-year-of-the-poet

and there is much, much more !

visit . . .

www.innerchildpress.com/antho
logies-sales-special.php

Also check out our Authors and
all the wonderful Books
Available at :

www.innerchildpress.com/autho
rs-pages

INNER CHILD PRESS

WORLD HEALING WORLD PEACE
2018

A Poetry Anthology for Humanity

Now Available

www.worldhealingworldpeacepoetry.com

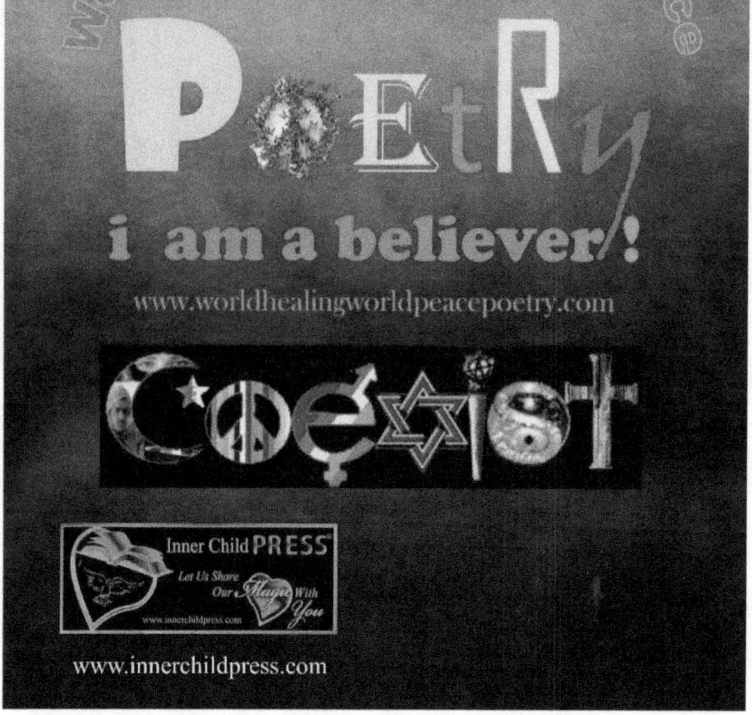

Now Available

www.worldhealingworldpeacepoetry.com

I support

World Healing World Peace

www.worldhealingworldpeacepoetry.com

World Healing
World Peace
2018

Now Available

www.worldhealingworldpeacepoetry.com

Inner Child Press International

'building bridges of cultural understanding'

Meet our Cultural Ambassadors

Fahredin Shehu
Director of Cultural

Faleha Hassan
Iraq - USA

Elizabeth E. Castillo
Philippines

Antoinette Coleman
Chicago
Midwest USA

Ananda Nepali
Nepal - Tibet
Northern Indea

Kimberly Burnham
Pacific Northwest
USA

Alicja Kuberska
Poland
Eastern Europe

Swapna Behera
India
Southeast Asia

Kolade O. Freedom
Nigeria
West Africa

Monsif Beroual
Morocco
Northern Africa

Ashok K. Bhargava
Canada

Tzemin Ition Tsai
Republic of China
Greater China

Alicia M. Ramírez
Mexico
Central America

Christena AV Williams
Jamaica
Caribbean

Louise Hudon
Eastern Canada

Aziz Mountassir
Morocco
Northern Africa

Shareef Abdur-Rasheed
Southeastern USA

Laure Churazac
France
Western Europe

Mohammud Ikbal Harb
Lebanon
Middle East

Mohamed Abdel
Aziz Shmeis
Egypt
Middle East

Hilary Maunga
Kenya
Eastern Africa

Josephus R. Johnson
Liberia

www.innerchildpress.com

This Anthological Publication
is underwritten solely by

Inner Child Press

Inner Child Press is a Publishing Company
Founded and Operated by Writers. Our
personal publishing experiences provides
us an intimate understanding of the
sometimes daunting challenges Writers,
New and Seasoned may face in the
Business of Publishing and Marketing
their Creative "Written Work".

For more Information

Inner Child Press

www.innerchildpress.com

Inner Child Press International

'building bridges of cultural understanding'

202 Wiltree Court, State College, Pennsylvania 16801

www.innerchildpress.com

~ *fini* ~

Coming
April 2020

Inner Child Press International

building bridges of cultural understanding
www.innerchildpress.com

The
World Healing, World Peace
International Poetry Symposium

Stay Tuned

for more information
intouch@innerchildpress.com
'building bridges of cultural understanding'
www.innerchildpress.com